THE CLASSIC
COCKTAIL
BIBLE

hamlyn

First published in Great Britain in 2012 by Spruce, an imprint of Octopus Publishing Group Ltd
Carmelite House
50 Victoria Embankment
London, EC4Y 0DZ
www.octopusbooks.co.uk
www.octopusbooks.usa.com

An Hachette UK Company
ww.hachette.co.uk

This edition published in 2023 by Hamlyn

Copyright © Octopus Publishing Group Ltd 2012

The recipes in this book were previously published in either 'The Cocktail Bible' or 'Cocktail', both published by Hamlyn.

Distributed in the US by Hachette Book Group
1290 Avenue of the Americas
4th and 5th Floors
New York, NY 10104

Distributed in Canada by
Canadian Manda Group
664 Annette Street
Toronto, Ontario, Canada M6S 2C8

ISBN 978-0-600-63802-5

A CIP catalogue record for this book is available from the British Library

Printed and bound in China

10 9 8 7 6 5 4 3 2 1

MIX
Paper | Supporting responsible forestry
FSC
www.fsc.org
FSC® C008047

NOTES

The measure that has been used in the recipes is based on a bar jigger, which is 25 ml (1 fl oz). If preferred, a different volume can be used providing the proportions are kept constant within a drink and suitable adjustments are made to spoon measurements, where they occur.

Standard level spoon measurements are used in all recipes.
1 tablespoon = one 15 ml spoon
1 teaspoon = one 5 ml spoon

Safety note
The Department of Health advises that eggs should not be consumed raw. This book contains recipes made with raw eggs. It is prudent for more vulnerable people, such as pregnant women, nursing mothers, invalids and the elderly to avoid these recipes.

THE **CLASSIC**
COCKTAIL
BIBLE

hamlyn

CONTENTS

INTRODUCTION

Who doesn't feel gorgeous and glamorous when they have an expertly mixed Martini in their hand? From the decadent 1920s, when bartenders took the sting out of Prohibition liquor by mixing it with more palatable flavours, to the over-indulgence of the 1980s and the cool cocktail chic of the noughties, cocktails have long had a part to play in party-people's social lives. With their exotic names, their indulgent ingredients and the care and attention required to create them, it's no surprise that these drinks have remained exclusive and exciting, and are constantly evolving.

ART IN A GLASS

Cocktails should taste every bit as good as they look, which is why bartenders spend years perfecting the art of the perfect blend of ingredients. Tiny tweaks to measurements can make all the difference, and a good cocktail is the result of careful measuring and mixing of very specific ingredients. So don't be tempted to simply empty all those leftover bottles of holiday booze into pretty glasses – cocktail making requires skill and precision, a basic knowledge of spirits and mixers, and a lightness of touch.

CLASSICS AND NEWCOMERS

The wonderful thing about cocktails is that classic recipes like the Martini, Zombie and Old-fashioned are as popular today as when they were first sipped in the lounge bars of fancy hotels around the world. These drinks have achieved cult status, but they're not too high and mighty to keep the newcomers banished from our bar menus. Mixologists are constantly creating new concoctions and the infinite combination of spirits, mixers, juices, syrups and decorations means that the only limit to the range of cocktails in a bar is the imagination of the bartender. But you don't need to flash your cash in a fancy joint to enjoy the glitz of a cocktail evening: you can create your own drinks at home. With a bit of forward planning, some essential equipment and a few choice recipes up your sleeve, you can become a mixologist for the night, and shake and stir to your heart's content.

VODKA

BAY BREEZE

- ice cubes
- 4 measures cranberry juice
- 2 measures vodka
- 2 measures pineapple juice
- lime wedges, to decorate

This is a variation of the classic Sea Breeze. Here, pineapple juice is used to add a touch of sweetness that contrasts with the piquant flavour of cranberries.

Fill a highball glass with ice cubes and pour over the cranberry juice. Pour the vodka and pineapple juice into a chilled cocktail shaker, shake well and gently pour over the cranberry juice and ice in the glass. Decorate with lime wedges and serve with long straws.

LE MANS (Pictured)

- 2–3 ice cubes, cracked
- 1 measure Cointreau
- ½ measure vodka
- soda water, to top up
- lemon wedge, to decorate

Put the cracked ice into a highball glass. Pour over the Cointreau and vodka, stir and top up with soda water. Float a lemon wedge on top of the drink and serve.

SCREWDRIVER

- 2–3 ice cubes
- 1½ measures vodka
- fresh orange juice, to top up

A popular drink that is a simple but delicious combination of vodka and orange juice. As the ingredients are minimal, it's important to use freshly squeezed juice.

Put the ice cubes into a highball glass. Pour over the vodka, top up with orange juice and stir lightly, then serve.

SEA BREEZE

- ice cubes
- 2 measures vodka
- 4 measures cranberry juice
- 2 measures fresh pink grapefruit juice
- 2 lime wedges

Put some ice cubes into a highball or hurricane glass. Pour over the vodka and fruit juices. Squeeze the lime wedges into the drink and stir lightly before serving.

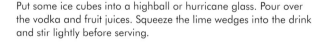

HARVEY WALLBANGER

- 6 ice cubes
- 1 measure vodka
- 3 measures fresh orange juice
- 1–2 teaspoons Galliano
- orange wheels, to decorate

This was named after a Californian surfer in the 1960s, who drank so many of this cocktail that he banged and bounced off the bar walls on his way out.

Put half the ice cubes into a cocktail shaker and the remainder into a highball glass. Add the vodka and orange juice to the shaker and shake until a frost forms on the outside of the shaker. Strain over the ice in the glass. Float the Galliano on top (see page 36). Decorate with orange wheels and serve with straws.

VODKA SAZERAC

- 1 white sugar cube
- 2 drops Angostura bitters
- 3 drops Pernod
- 2–3 ice cubes
- 2 measures vodka
- lemonade, to top up

Put the sugar cube into a rocks glass and shake the bitters on to it. Add the Pernod and swirl it around to coat the inside of the glass. Add the ice cubes and pour over the vodka. Top up with lemonade and stir lightly, then serve.

BLOODY MARY (Pictured)

- ice cubes
- 2 measures vodka
- 1 dash fresh lemon juice
- Worcestershire sauce, to taste
- tomato juice, to top up
- ½ teaspoon cayenne pepper
- salt and pepper
- celery stalks, to decorate

The legendary 'Pete' Petoit, who worked at the famous Harry's New York Bar in Paris after World War I, was the inventor of the Bloody Mary.

Put some ice cubes into a highball glass. Pour over the vodka and lemon juice, add Worcestershire sauce to taste and top up with tomato juice. Add the cayenne pepper and season to taste with salt and pepper. Stir to chill. Decorate with celery stalks and serve.

BLUE MOON

- 5–6 ice cubes, cracked
- ¾ measure vodka
- ¾ measure tequila
- 1 measure blue Curaçao
- lemonade, to top up

Put half the cracked ice into a mixing glass. Add the vodka, tequila and blue Curaçao and stir to mix. Put the remaining ice into a tall glass and strain in the cocktail. Top up with lemonade and serve with a straw.

VODKA COLLINS

- 6 ice cubes
- 2 measures vodka
- juice of 1 lime
- 1 teaspoon caster sugar
- soda water, to top up
- lemon or lime wheels and a maraschino cherry, to decorate

The Collins takes its name from its creator, John Collins. He first mixed the drink in the early 19th century at Limmer's Hotel in London.

Put half the ice cubes into a cocktail shaker. Add the vodka, lime juice and sugar and shake until a frost forms on the outside of the shaker. Strain into a large highball glass, add the remaining ice cubes and top up with soda water. Decorate with lemon or lime wheels and a maraschino cherry and serve.

COSMOPOLITAN (Pictured)

- 6 ice cubes, cracked
- 1 measure vodka
- ½ measure Cointreau
- 1 measure cranberry juice
- juice of ½ lime
- orange rind twist, to decorate

Put the cracked ice into a cocktail shaker. Add all the remaining ingredients and shake until a frost forms on the outside of the shaker. Strain into a chilled Martini glass. Decorate with an orange rind twist and serve.

MOSCOW MULE

- 3–4 ice cubes, cracked
- 2 measures vodka
- juice of 2 limes
- ginger beer, to top up
- lime or orange wheels, to decorate

This was invented in 1941 by an employee of a US drinks firm in conjunction with a Los Angeles bar owner who was overstocked with ginger beer.

Put the cracked ice into a cocktail shaker. Add the vodka and lime juice and shake until a frost forms on the outside of the shaker. Pour, without straining, into a highball glass, top up with ginger beer and stir lightly. Decorate with lime or orange wheels and serve.

GREEN ISLAND QUIET SUNDAY

- 4–6 ice cubes, plus crushed ice to serve
- 1 measure vodka
- 4 measures orange juice
- 3 dashes Amaretto di Saronno
- few drops of grenadine

Put the ice cubes with the vodka, orange juice and Amaretto into a cocktail shaker and shake well. Strain into a highball glass filled with crushed ice, then add a few drops of grenadine.

XANTIPPE

- 4–5 ice cubes
- 1 measure cherry brandy
- 1 measure Yellow Chartreuse
- 2 measures vodka

Chartreuse is a herb-based liqueur named after a Carthusian monastery near Grenoble in France where it was first made. Yellow Chartreuse has a lower alcohol content than Green Chartreuse.

Put the ice cubes into a mixing glass. Pour over the cherry brandy, Chartreuse and vodka and stir vigorously. Strain into a chilled Martini glass, then serve.

NEW DAY (Pictured)

- 4–5 ice cubes
- 3 measures vodka
- 1 measure Calvados
- 1 measure apricot brandy
- juice of ½ orange
- orange wedge, to decorate

Put the ice cubes into a cocktail shaker. Add all the remaining ingredients and shake until a frost forms on the outside of the shaker. Strain into a rocks glass, decorate with an orange wedge and serve.

DAWA

- 1 lime, quartered and thickly sliced
- 1 tablespoon thick honey
- 1 teaspoon caster sugar
- 2–3 ice cubes
- 2 measures vodka

The Swahili word *dawa* means something between a medicine and a magic potion. It is traditionally served with a wooden muddler to release more lime juice and adjust the flavour.

Put the lime slices, honey and sugar into a rocks glass and muddle together (see page 37). Add the ice cubes and pour over the vodka, then serve.

GINGERSNAP

- 2–3 ice cubes
- 3 measures vodka
- 1 measure ginger wine
- soda water, to top up

Put the ice cubes into a rocks glass. Pour over the vodka and ginger wine and stir lightly. Top up with soda water and serve.

WHITE RUSSIAN

- 6 ice cubes, cracked
- 1 measure vodka
- 1 measure Tia Maria
- 1 measure full-fat milk or double cream

This modern take on the Black Russian uses Tia Maria and cream to give the drink its distinctive colour and texture.

Put half the cracked ice into a cocktail shaker and put the remaining cracked ice into a highball glass. Add all the remaining ingredients to the shaker and shake until a frost forms on the outside of the shaker. Strain over the ice in the glass. Serve with a straw.

PARROT'S HEAD PUNCH (Pictured)

- ice cubes
- 1½ measures vodka
- 1 measure passion fruit liqueur
- 2 measures watermelon juice
- 1 measure cranberry juice
- 1½ measures fresh pink grapefruit juice
- pink grapefruit wheel, to decorate

Fill a hurricane glass with ice cubes. Build all the remaining ingredients, one by one in order, over the ice and decorate with a pink grapefruit wheel. Serve with long straws.

BLACK RUSSIAN

- 4–6 ice cubes, cracked
- 2 measures vodka
- 1 measure Kahlúa
- chocolate stick, to decorate (optional)

This is the original cocktail, dating back to the 1950s. Nowadays, it is often served as a long drink, topped up with chilled cola.

Put the cracked ice into a rocks glass. Pour over the vodka and Kahlúa and stir. Decorate with a chocolate stick, if you like, and serve.

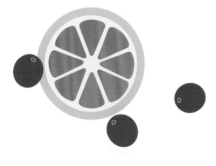

SEX ON THE BEACH

- ice cubes
- 1 measure vodka
- 1 measure peach schnapps
- 1 measure cranberry juice
- 1 measure orange juice
- 1 measure pineapple juice (optional)
- orange and lime slices, to decorate

Put some ice cubes into a cocktail shaker and add the vodka, schnapps, cranberry juice, orange juice and pineapple juice, if using. Shake well. Pour over 3–4 ice cubes in a tall glass, decorate with the orange and lime slices and serve with straws.

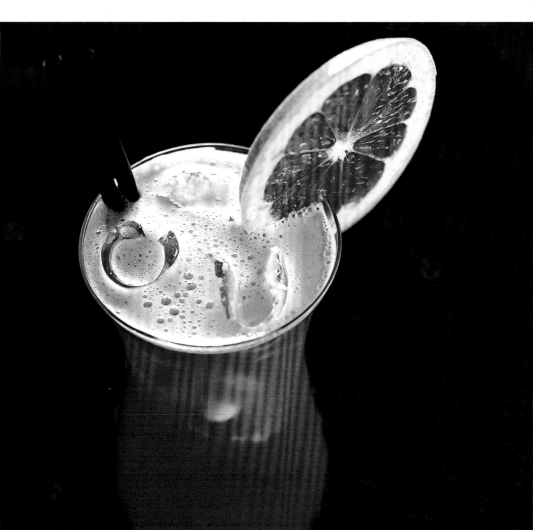

CAPE CODDER

- ice cubes
- 2 measures vodka
- 4 measures cranberry juice
- 6 lime wedges, to decorate

This long drink gained in popularity with the vogue for cranberry juice. Cape Cod in Massachusetts is responsible for much of the USA's cranberry production.

Fill a highball glass with ice cubes. Pour over the vodka and cranberry juice, then squeeze half the lime wedges into the drink. Stir well, decorate with the remaining lime wedges and serve with a straw, if you like.

MARGUERITE

- 4–5 ice cubes, plus cracked ice to serve
- 3 measures vodka
- juice of 1 lemon
- juice of ½ orange
- raspberry syrup, maraschino liqueur or grenadine, to taste

Put the ice cubes into a cocktail shaker. Pour the vodka, fruit juices and raspberry syrup, maraschino liqueur or grenadine over the ice. Shake until a frost forms. Strain into a rocks glass filled with cracked ice.

SWALLOW DIVE (Pictured)

- ice cubes, plus crushed ice to serve
- 1 measure honey vodka
- 1 measure Chambord
- 1 measure lime juice
- 4 raspberries, plus 2 to decorate

Chambord is a rich but delicate liqueur, made from red and black raspberries, honey, vanilla, citrus peel and cognac.

Put some ice cubes with all the other ingredients into a cocktail shaker. Shake well. Strain over crushed ice in a rocks glass. Top up with more crushed ice and decorate with the 2 extra raspberries.

HAIR RAISER

- 1–2 ice cubes, cracked
- 1 measure vodka
- 1 measure sweet vermouth
- 1 measure tonic water
- lemon and lime rind spirals, to decorate

Put the cracked ice into a tall glass and pour over the vodka, vermouth and tonic water. Stir lightly. Decorate with the lemon and lime rind spirals and serve with a straw.

SURF RIDER (Pictured)

- 4–5 ice cubes
- 3 measures vodka
- 1 measure sweet vermouth
- juice of ½ lemon
- juice of 1 orange
- ½ teaspoon grenadine

Grenadine is a red, non-alcoholic syrup made from pomegranates. As well as imparting a lovely rich colour to drinks, it adds a fruity flavour.

Put the ice cubes into a cocktail shaker. Pour the vodka, vermouth, fruit juices and grenadine over the ice. Shake until a frost forms. Strain and pour into a sour glass.

HAVEN

- ice cubes
- 1 tablespoon grenadine
- 1 measure Pernod
- 1 measure vodka
- soda water, to top up

Put 2–3 ice cubes in a rocks glass. Dash the grenadine over the ice, then pour in the Pernod and vodka. Top up with soda water.

HERBERT LEE

- 4–5 ice cubes
- 2 measures vodka
- 1 measure Calvados
- 1 teaspoon crème de cassis

You can make a Davey-Davey by replacing the crème de cassis in this recipe with the juice of half a grapefruit.

Put the ice cubes into a mixing glass. Pour the vodka, Calvados and crème de cassis over the ice. Stir vigorously, then strain into a chilled Martini glass.

FRENCH LEAVE

- ice cubes
- 1 measure orange juice
- 1 measure vodka
- 1 measure Pernod

Put some ice cubes with all the other ingredients into a cocktail shaker and shake well. Strain into a Martini glass.

PDQ

- 4–5 ice cubes
- 1½ measures chilli-flavoured vodka
- 1 measure vodka
- 2 measures chilled beef bouillon
- 1 tablespoon fresh lemon juice
- dash of Tabasco sauce
- dash of Worcestershire sauce
- salt and black pepper
- lemon slice and bottled chilli, to decorate

Tabasco sauce is a spicy sauce made with chilli peppers – it's fiery, so add with caution!

Put the ice cubes into a cocktail shaker. Pour the vodkas, bouillon and lemon juice over the ice and dash in the Tabasco and Worcestershire sauces. Shake until a frost forms, then strain into a hurricane glass. Season to taste with salt and pepper and decorate with a slice of lemon and a chilli.

RISING SUN

- ice cubes
- 2 measures vodka
- 2 teaspoons passion fruit syrup
- 3 measures grapefruit juice
- pink grapefruit slice, to decorate

Put some of the ice cubes with the vodka, passion fruit syrup and grapefruit juice into a shaker and shake to mix. Strain into a rocks glass over 6–8 ice cubes. Decorate with a pink grapefruit slice.

BELLINI-TINI (Pictured)

- 4–5 ice cubes, cracked
- 2 measures vodka
- ½ measure peach schnapps
- 1 teaspoon peach juice
- chilled Champagne, to top up
- peach slices, to decorate

The Bellini was first created in Harry's Bar in Venice about 70 years ago. The bartender named his drink after the Italian artist Giovanni Bellini.

Put the cracked ice into a cocktail shaker. Add the vodka, schnapps and peach juice and shake until a frost forms on the outside of the shaker. Strain into a chilled Martini glass and top up with chilled Champagne. Decorate with peach slices and serve.

COOL WIND

- 4–5 ice cubes
- 1 measure dry vermouth
- ½ teaspoon Cointreau
- 3 measures vodka
- juice of ½ grapefruit

Put the ice cubes into a mixing glass. Pour the vermouth, Cointreau, vodka and grapefruit juice over the ice. Stir gently, then strain into a chilled Martini glass.

VODKA CAIPIROSKA

- 6 lime wedges
- 2 teaspoons soft light brown sugar
- 2 measures vodka
- crushed ice

This is a vodka variation of the authentic Caipirinha cocktail (see page 164), which traditionally features cachaça, a Brazilian spirit made from rum and sugar cane.

Put half the lime wedges, the sugar and vodka into a highball or rocks glass and muddle together (see page 37). Top up with crushed ice. Decorate with the remaining lime wedges and serve.

VODKA DAIQUIRI

- 6 ice cubes, cracked
- 1 measure vodka
- 1 teaspoon caster sugar
- juice of ½ lime or lemon

Put the cracked ice into a cocktail shaker. Add all the remaining ingredients and shake until a frost forms on the outside of the shaker. Strain into a Martini glass and serve.

KIWI CAIPIROSKA (Pictured)

- ½ kiwifruit, peeled
- ½ lime, cut into wedges
- 2 teaspoons sugar syrup (see page 122)
- crushed ice
- 2 measures vodka
- 2 teaspoons kiwifruit schnapps

Featuring on the menu of cocktail bars throughout Brazil, Argentina and Uruguay, a Caipiroska is also sometimes known as a Caipivodka.

Put the kiwifruit, lime wedges and sugar syrup into a rocks glass and muddle together (see page 37). Fill the glass with crushed ice, pour over the vodka and stir. Add more ice, then drizzle the schnapps over the surface.

VANILLA VODKA SOUR

- 4–5 ice cubes
- 2 measures vanilla vodka
- ½ measure sugar syrup (see page 122)
- 1 egg white
- 1½ measures fresh lemon juice
- 3 drops Angostura bitters, to decorate

Put the ice cubes into a cocktail shaker. Add the vodka, sugar syrup, egg white and lemon juice and shake until a frost forms on the outside of the shaker. Pour, without straining, into a Martini glass and shake the Angostura bitters on top to decorate.

FLOWER POWER SOUR

- ice cubes
- 1½ measures Absolut Mandarin Vodka
- ½ measure Mandarine Napoléon
- 2 teaspoons elderflower cordial
- 2 teaspoons sugar syrup (see page 122)
- 1 measure fresh lemon juice
- orange rind spiral, to decorate

This is an unusual, fresh and fragrant Sour, made with vodka flavoured with Mandarine Napoléon, a liqueur infused with mandarin rind, and elderflower cordial.

Half-fill a cocktail shaker with ice cubes and fill a rocks glass with ice cubes. Add all the remaining ingredients to the shaker and shake until a frost forms on the outside of the shaker. Strain over the ice in the glass. Decorate with an orange rind spiral and serve.

GLAMOUR MARTINI (Pictured)

- ice cubes
- 1½ measures vodka
- ½ measure cherry brandy
- 2 measures fresh blood orange juice
- ½ measure fresh lime juice
- orange rind twist, to decorate

Half-fill a cocktail shaker with ice cubes. Add all the remaining ingredients and shake until a frost forms on the outside of the shaker. Strain into a chilled Martini glass. Decorate with an orange rind twist and serve.

VODKATINI

- 5–6 ice cubes
- 3 measures chilled vodka
- ½ measure Noilly Prat
- olives, to decorate

Known as 'the Rolls-Royce of vermouths', Noilly Prat is dry vermouth infused with herbs and spices, including coriander, cloves and nutmeg.

Put the ice cubes into a mixing glass. Pour over the vodka and Noilly Prat and stir vigorously and evenly without splashing. Strain into a chilled Martini glass. Decorate with olives and serve.

APPLE MARTINI

- ice cubes
- 2 measures vodka
- 1 measure apple schnapps
- 1 tablespoon apple purée
- 1 dash freshly squeezed lime juice
- pinch of ground cinnamon
- red apple wedges, to decorate

Half-fill a cocktail shaker with ice cubes. Add all the remaining ingredients and shake until a frost forms on the outside of the shaker. Fine or double strain (see page 66) into a chilled Martini glass. Decorate with red apple wedges and serve.

ICEBERG

- 4–6 ice cubes
- 1½ measures vodka
- 1 dash Pernod

Pernod is probably the best known of the pastis – French aniseed-flavoured spirits that are drunk as an aperitif.

Put the ice cubes into a rocks glass. Pour over the vodka and add the Pernod, then serve.

KITSCH REVOLT (Pictured)

- ice cubes
- 1 measure Absolut Kurant Vodka
- ½ measure strawberry purée
- 5 measures chilled Champagne
- strawberry, to decorate

Half-fill a cocktail shaker with ice cubes. Add the vodka and strawberry purée and shake briefly to mix. Strain into a Martini glass. Top up with the chilled Champagne and stir. Decorate with a strawberry and serve.

VODKA GRASSHOPPER

- crushed ice
- 1½ measures vodka
- 1½ measures green crème de menthe
- 1½ measures white crème de cacao

Crème de menthe gives this cocktail its distinctive green colour, hence the name Grasshopper.

Half-fill a cocktail shaker with crushed ice. Add all the remaining ingredients and shake until a frost forms on the outside of the shaker. Strain into a chilled Martini glass and serve.

FEDERATION

- 4–5 ice cubes
- 3 drops orange or Angostura bitters
- 2 measures vodka
- 1 measure port

Put the ice cubes into a mixing glass. Shake the bitters over the ice. Add the vodka and port. Stir vigorously and strain into a chilled Martini glass.

SHAKE IT LIKE A MIXOLOGIST

If you want your cocktails to taste as good as a prize-winning mixologist's, then you need to perfect a few techniques. Each drink is prepared differently, in order to mix the ingredients together perfectly and achieve the best possible flavour.

STIRRING

This requires a gentle touch and is used for drinks that need to be chilled but remain clear.

- Add the ingredients to the cocktail glass or a mixing glass.
- Use a bar spoon to lightly stir the ingredients together – this will sometimes be with ice, to chill the drink at the same time.
- Pour the drink into the cocktail glass (if prepared in a mixing glass) and finish with a decoration.

SHAKING

This is fairly simple but you need a strong wrist to really combine the ingredients and ensure the cocktail is well chilled.

- Half-fill the cocktail shaker with ice cubes or crushed ice (depending on the recipe). Chill the glass.
- Add the ingredients to the shaker, put the cap on and shake until there's condensation on the outside of the shaker.
- Strain the drink into the prepared cocktail glass.

LAYERING

This is a clever technique that is often used in shots. Basically, the heaviest liquid is added to the glass first, followed by the remaining ingredients, one by one, to create multi-coloured layers in the glass.

- Add the first ingredient, as listed in the recipe, pouring carefully into the centre of the glass.
- Now, place a bar spoon in the centre of the glass, and add the second liquid. This will run down the bar spoon and sit on top of the first liquid.
- When you've finished all the layers, remove the bar spoon and serve.

MUDDLING

The Mojito is probably the best-known muddled drink, although others are also prepared in this way.

- Pull the mint leaves from the stems and put in the base of a highball glass.
- Add sugar syrup and lime wedges.
- Use the muddler to push down on the ingredients for about 30 seconds, extracting as much juice and flavour as possible.
- Top up the glass with crushed ice and add the spirit and mixer, according to the recipe.

WHITE SPIDER

- 2 measures vodka
- 1 measure white crème de menthe
- crushed ice (optional)

Crème de menthe is a sweet, mint-flavoured liqueur which is available in a green and white, or clear, version.

Pour the vodka and crème de menthe into a cocktail shaker. Shake well, then pour into a chilled Martini glass or over crushed ice.

SCOTCH FROG

- ice cubes
- 2 measures vodka
- 1 measure Galliano
- 1 measure Cointreau
- juice of 1 lime
- 1 dash Angostura bitters
- 2 dashes maraschino cherry syrup

Fill a cocktail shaker three-quarters full with ice cubes. Add all the other ingredients, shake well and strain into a chilled Martini glass.

PARSON'S NOSE

- 2 measures vodka
- ½ measure Amaretto di Saronno
- ½ measure crème de peche
- 1 measure Angostura bitters

Sweet and with a pronounced flavour of ripe peaches, crème de peche is one of the more unusual fruit liqueurs.

Stir the ingredients in a mixing glass, then strain into a chilled Martini glass and serve.

DECATINI (Pictured)

- ice cubes
- 2 measures raspberry vodka
- ½ measure chocolate syrup, plus extra to decorate
- ½ measure double cream
- 1 measure morello cherry purée

Half-fill a cocktail shaker with ice cubes. Add the vodka, chocolate syrup and half the cream and shake until a frost forms on the outside of the shaker. Strain into a chilled Martini glass. Wash out the shaker, then add the cherry purée and the remaining cream and shake briefly to mix. Float the cherry liquid over the chocolate liquid in the glass (see page 36). Decorate with a swirl of chocolate syrup and serve.

HORIZON (Pictured)

- ice cubes
- 1½ measures Zubrowka Vodka
- ½ measure Xante pear liqueur
- 1 measure pressed apple juice
- 1 teaspoon passion fruit liqueur
- 1 dash lemon juice
- pared lemon rind, to decorate

Zubrowka is a Polish vodka that's made from rye grain and bison grass. It has recently gained an increased following among drinkers and bartenders.

Half-fill a cocktail shaker with ice cubes. Add all the remaining ingredients and shake until a frost forms on the outside of the shaker. Fine or double strain (see page 66) into a chilled Martini glass. Decorate with pared lemon rind and serve.

POLISH MARTINI

- ice cubes
- 1 measure Zubrowka Vodka
- 1 measure Krupnik Vodka
- 1 measure Wyborowa Vodka (standard Polish)
- 1 measure apple juice
- lemon rind twist, to decorate

Put some ice cubes into a mixing glass. Pour over the three vodkas and the apple juice and stir well. Strain into a chilled Martini glass. Decorate with a lemon rind twist and serve.

BLACKBERRY MARTINI

- 2 measures Absolut Kurant Vodka
- 1 measure crème de mûre
- ice cubes
- blackberry, to decorate

The powerful flavours of this Martini are provided by Absolut Kurant, a blackcurrant-flavoured vodka, and crème de mûre, a blackberry liqueur.

Put the vodka and crème de mûre into a mixing glass, add some ice cubes and stir well. Strain into a chilled Martini glass. Decorate with a single blackberry and serve.

KATINKA

- ice cubes
- 1½ measures vodka
- 1 measure apricot brandy
- 2 teaspoons fresh lime juice
- mint sprig, to decorate

Half-fill a cocktail shaker with ice cubes. Add all the remaining ingredients and shake until a frost forms on the outside of the shaker. Strain into a Martini glass. Decorate with a mint sprig and serve.

KAMIKAZE

- 6 ice cubes, cracked
- ½ measure vodka
- ½ measure triple sec
- ½ measure fresh lime juice

Developed in the 19th century and originally called Curaçao triple sec, triple sec is a colourless, orange-flavoured variety of Curaçao.

Put the cracked ice into a cocktail shaker. Add all the remaining ingredients and shake until a frost forms on the outside of the shaker. Strain into a shot glass and serve.

PILLOW TALK (Pictured)

- ½ measure chilled strawberry vodka
- ½ measure Mozart white chocolate liqueur
- 1 squirt aerosol cream

Using a bar spoon, carefully layer the vodka and white chocolate liqueur in a shot glass (see page 36). Add a squirt of aerosol cream, then serve.

ROCK CHICK

- ice cubes
- 1 measure Absolut Kurant Vodka
- 1 dash peach schnapps
- 1 dash fresh lime juice

Schnapps is a clear liquor distilled from fermented fruit. The five types of fruit used to make schnapps are apples, pears, cherries, apricots and peaches.

Half-fill a cocktail shaker with ice cubes. Add all the remaining ingredients and shake briefly to mix. Strain into a shot glass and serve.

KIWI-TINI

- ½ kiwifruit, peeled
- ¼ measure sugar syrup (see page 122)
- ice cubes
- 2 measures vodka
- ¼ measure kiwifruit schnapps
- kiwifruit wheel, to decorate

Put the kiwifruit and sugar syrup into a mixing glass and muddle together (see page 37). Half-fill a cocktail shaker with ice cubes. Add the kiwifruit mixture and all the remaining ingredients and shake until a frost forms on the outside of the shaker. Strain into a chilled Martini glass. Fine or double strain (see page 66) if you want to remove all the kiwifruit pips, although they look good left in. Decorate with a kiwifruit wheel and serve.

RUM

KINKY WITCH

- ice cubes
- 1 measure Havana Club 3-year-old rum
- 1 measure Havana Club Silver Dry rum
- ½ measure orange Curaçao
- ½ measure crème de mûre
- ½ measure orgeat syrup
- 2 measures orange juice
- 2 measures grapefruit juice
- 2 teaspoons over-proof rum
- grapefruit wedges, to decorate

This cocktail contains orgeat syrup, a sweet syrup that is made from almonds, sugar and rose- or orange-flower water and is non-alcoholic.

Put some ice cubes with the Havana Club rums, Curaçao, crème de mûre, orgeat syrup and fruit juices into a cocktail shaker and shake well. Strain into a highball glass filled with ice cubes, float the over-proof rum over the surface (see page 36) and decorate with grapefruit wedges.

HAVANA ZOMBIE

- 4–5 ice cubes
- juice of 1 lime
- 5 tablespoons pineapple juice
- 1 teaspoon sugar syrup (see page 122)
- 1 measure white rum
- 1 measure golden rum
- 1 measure dark rum

Put the ice cubes into a mixing glass. Pour the fruit juices, sugar syrup and rums over the ice and stir vigorously. Pour the cocktail without straining into a tall glass.

ZOMBIE

- ice cubes
- 1 measure dark rum
- 1 measure white rum
- ½ measure golden rum
- ½ measure apricot brandy
- juice of ½ lime
- 1 teaspoon grenadine
- 2 measures pineapple juice
- ½ measure sugar syrup (see page 122)
- 2 teaspoons over-proof rum
- pineapple wedge and leaf and sugar, to decorate

Said to have been named for the effect it had on drinkers, the Zombie first appeared in the late 1930s at Don the Beachcomber, a popular Polynesian-themed restaurant in Hollywood.

Put some ice cubes with the first 3 rums, apricot brandy, lime juice, grenadine, pineapple juice and sugar syrup into a cocktail shaker and shake well. Pour into a chilled glass without straining and float the over-proof rum on top (see page 36). Decorate with a pineapple wedge and leaf, and sprinkle a pinch of sugar over the top.

ZOMBIE PRINCE (Pictured)

- crushed ice
- juice of 1 lemon
- juice of 1 orange
- juice of ½ grapefruit
- 3 drops Angostura bitters
- 1 teaspoon soft
  brown sugar
- 1 measure white rum
- 1 measure golden rum
- 1 measure dark rum
- lime and orange slices,
  to decorate

Put the crushed ice into a mixing glass. Pour the fruit juices over the ice and splash in the bitters. Add the sugar and pour in the rums. Stir vigorously, then pour without straining into a tall glass. Decorate with lime and orange slices.

MONOLOCO ZOMBIE (Pictured)

- ice cubes
- 1 measure white rum
- 1 measure Navy Rum
- ½ measure apricot brandy
- ½ measure orange Curaçao
- 2 measures orange juice
- 2 measures pineapple juice
- ½ measure fresh lime juice
- 1 dash grenadine
- ½ measure over-proof rum
- pineapple wedges, to decorate

Over-proof rum is a high-strength, potent rum which is mostly used in layered cocktails as a 'floating' top layer.

Put some ice cubes with all the other ingredients, except the over-proof rum, into a cocktail shaker. Shake well. Strain over ice cubes in a large hurricane glass. Top with the over-proof rum and decorate with pineapple wedges.

NEW ORLEANS DANDY

- 4–5 ice cubes
- 1 measure white rum
- ½ measure peach brandy
- 1 dash fresh orange juice
- 1 dash fresh lime juice
- Champagne, to top up

Put the ice cubes into a cocktail shaker. Pour the rum, peach brandy and fruit juices over the ice and shake until a frost forms. Strain the cocktail into a Champagne flute or tall glass and top up with Champagne.

SERENADE

- 6 ice cubes, crushed
- 1 measure white rum
- ½ measure Amaretto di Saronno
- ½ measure coconut cream
- 2 measures pineapple juice
- pineapple slice, to decorate

The origin of the word 'rum' isn't certain, although one theory is that it comes from 'rumbullion', which means 'a great tumult or uproar'.

Put half the ice into a food processor or blender, add the rum, Amaretto, coconut cream and pineapple juice and blend for 20 seconds. Pour into a tall glass over the remaining ice cubes. Decorate with a pineapple slice and serve with a straw.

TIKI TREAT

- crushed ice
- ½ ripe mango, peeled and stoned, plus extra to decorate
- 3 coconut chunks
- 1 measure coconut cream
- 2 measures aged rum
- dash fresh lemon juice
- 1 teaspoon caster sugar

Put a small scoop of crushed ice with all the other ingredients into a food processor or blender and blend until smooth. Serve in a hurricane glass with long straws and decorate with mango slices.

MOJITO (Pictured)

- 12 mint leaves, plus an extra sprig to decorate
- ½ measure sugar syrup (see page 122)
- 4 lime wedges
- crushed ice
- 2 measures white rum
- soda water, to top up

This is a cooling, effervescent cocktail born – thanks to Prohibition – amid Cuba's thriving international bar culture. It probably derived from the Mint Julep (see page 114).

Put the mint, sugar syrup and lime wedges into a highball glass and muddle together (see page 37). Fill the glass with crushed ice, pour over the rum and stir. Top up with soda water. Decorate with a mint sprig and serve with straws.

PINK MOJITO

- 6 mint leaves, plus an extra sprig to decorate
- ½ lime, cut into wedges
- 2 teaspoons sugar syrup (see page 122)
- 3 raspberries
- crushed ice
- 1½ measures white rum
- ½ measure Chambord
- cranberry juice, to top up

All types of Mojito, including this pink-hued one, use mint leaves. The original Cuban recipe uses *yerba buena*, a type of spearmint popular on the island.

Put the mint leaves, lime wedges, sugar syrup and raspberries into a highball glass and muddle together (see page 37). Add some crushed ice, then pour over the rum and Chambord. Stir well and top up with cranberry juice. Decorate with a mint sprig and serve.

LIMON MOJITO

- 1 lime, quartered
- 2 teaspoons soft brown sugar
- 8 mint leaves
- crushed ice
- 2 measures Bacardi Limon rum
- soda water, to top up (optional)
- lemon and lime slices, to decorate

Muddle the lime quarters, sugar and mint in a highball glass (see page 37). Fill the glass with crushed ice and add the rum. Stir and top up with soda water, if you like. Decorate with lemon and lime slices and serve with straws.

ST JAMES

- 3–4 ice cubes
- juice of ½ lime or lemon
- juice of 1 orange
- 3 drops Angostura bitters
- 2 measures white or golden rum
- 2 measures tonic water
- lime or lemon slice, to decorate

First produced in the town of Angostura in Venezuela as a cure for sea sickness, Angostura bitters is a key ingredient in numerous cocktails.

Put the ice cubes into a highball glass and pour in the fruit juices. Shake the bitters over the ice cubes, add the rum and tonic water and decorate with a lime or lemon slice. Stir gently.

PINEAPPLE MOJITO (Pictured)

- 6 mint leaves
- 4 pineapple chunks
- 2 teaspoons soft brown sugar
- 2 measures golden rum
- crushed ice
- pineapple juice, to top up
- pineapple wedge and mint sprig, to decorate

Muddle the mint leaves, pineapple chunks and sugar in a cocktail shaker (see page 37). Add the rum and shake well. Strain into a glass filled with crushed ice, top up with pineapple juice and stir. Decorate with a pineapple wedge and a mint sprig.

MAI TAI

- ice cubes
- crushed ice
- 2 measures golden rum
- ½ measure orange Curaçao
- ½ measure orgeat syrup
- juice of 1 lime
- 2 teaspoons Wood's Navy Rum
- lime rind spiral and mint sprig, to decorate

This cocktail, which takes its name from the Tahitian word *maita'i*, meaning 'good', is thought to have been invented at Trader Vic's restaurant in Oakland, California in 1944.

Half-fill a cocktail shaker with ice cubes and put some crushed ice into a rocks glass. Add the golden rum, Curaçao, orgeat syrup and lime juice to the shaker and shake until a frost forms on the outside of the shaker. Strain over the ice in the glass. Float the Navy Rum on top (see page 36). Decorate with a lime rind spiral and a mint sprig and serve.

HAVANA BEACH

- ½ lime
- 2 measures pineapple juice
- 1 measure white rum
- 1 teaspoon sugar
- dry ginger ale, to top up
- lime slice, to decorate

Cut the lime into 4 pieces and put in a food processor or blender with the pineapple juice, rum and sugar. Blend until smooth. Pour into a hurricane glass and top up with dry ginger ale. Decorate with a lime slice.

HUMMINGBIRD

- 4–5 ice cubes, crushed
- 1 measure dark rum
- 1 measure light rum
- 1 measure Southern Comfort
- 1 measure fresh orange juice
- cola, to top up
- orange slice, to decorate

Created by bartender Martin Wilkes Heron in New Orleans in 1874, Southern Comfort is a liqueur containing whiskey flavouring, along with fruit and spices.

Put the crushed ice into a cocktail shaker. Pour the rums, Southern Comfort and orange juice over the ice and shake until a frost forms. Strain into a long glass and top up with cola. Decorate with an orange slice and serve with a straw.

BOSSANOVA (Pictured)

- ice cubes
- 2 measures white rum
- ½ measure Galliano
- ½ measure apricot brandy
- 4 measures pressed apple juice
- 1 measure fresh lime juice
- ½ measure sugar syrup (see page 122)
- lime wedges, split, to decorate

Put some ice cubes with the rum, Galliano, apricot brandy, fruit juices and syrup into a cocktail shaker and shake well. Strain into a highball glass filled with ice cubes. Decorate with split lime wedges and serve with long straws.

PLANTER'S PUNCH

- ice cubes
- 2 measures Myer's Jamaican Planter's Punch Rum
- 4 drops Angostura bitters
- ½ measure fresh lime juice
- 2 measures iced water
- 1 measure sugar syrup (see page 122)
- orange and lime wheels, to decorate

This was created by Fred L Myers in the late 19th century. For a modern fruity version, substitute pineapple juice for the water.

Half-fill a cocktail shaker with ice cubes and fill a highball glass with ice cubes. Add all the remaining ingredients to the shaker and shake until a frost forms on the outside of the shaker. Strain over the ice in the glass. Decorate with orange and lime wheels and serve.

SPICED MULE

- ice cubes
- 8 measures Morgan Spiced Rum
- 2 measures fresh lime juice
- 2 measures sugar syrup (see page 122)
- 1 litre (1¾ pints) ginger beer, to top up
- lime wedges, to decorate

Half-fill the cocktail shaker with ice cubes and fill 6 highball glasses with ice cubes. Add the rum, lime juice and sugar syrup to the shaker and shake until a frost forms on the outside of the shaker. Pour into a large glass jug. Add more ice and top with ginger beer while stirring. Pour over the ice in the glasses, decorate with lime wedges and serve.

CUBA LIBRE

- ice cubes
- 4 measures golden rum, such as Havana Club 3-year-old
- juice of 1 lime
- cola, to top up
- lime wedges

There are many versions of the origins of the Cuba Libre. One is that fighters aiding Cuba in the Spanish-American War at the beginning of the 20th century would raise their glasses of rum and cola in a toast of 'Cuba Libre' ('Free Cuba').

Fill 2 highball glasses with ice cubes. Pour over the rum and lime juice and stir. Top up with cola, decorate with lime wedges and serve with straws.

ST LUCIA (Pictured)

- 4–5 ice cubes
- 1 measure Curaçao
- 1 measure dry vermouth
- juice of ½ orange
- 1 teaspoon grenadine
- 2 measures white or golden rum
- orange rind spiral and cocktail cherry, to decorate

Put the ice cubes into a cocktail shaker and pour over the Curaçao, vermouth, orange juice, grenadine and rum. Shake until a frost forms, then pour without straining into a highball glass. Decorate with an orange rind spiral and a cherry.

CUBAN BREEZE

- ice cubes
- 3 measures cranberry juice
- 2 measures golden rum, such as Havana Club 3-year-old
- 2 measures fresh grapefruit juice
- lime wedges, to decorate

You should invest in a good-quality aged rum to create a beautifully mellow drink.

Fill a highball glass with ice cubes and pour over the cranberry juice. Half-fill a cocktail shaker with ice cubes. Add the rum and grapefruit juice and shake until a frost forms on the outside of the shaker. Strain over the cranberry juice and ice in the glass. Decorate with lime wedges and serve.

JOLLY ROGER

- 5 ice cubes, cracked
- 1 measure dark rum
- 1 measure Galliano
- ½ measure apricot brandy
- 3 measures fresh orange juice
- apricot, orange and lemon slices, to decorate

Put half the cracked ice with the rum, Galliano, apricot brandy and orange juice into a cocktail shaker and shake well. Strain over the remaining ice into a tall glass. Decorate with the fruit slices.

THE PAPA DOBLE (Pictured)

- crushed ice
- 3 measures white rum
- ½ measure maraschino liqueur
- 1 measure fresh lime juice
- 1½ measures fresh grapefruit juice
- grapefruit wedge, to decorate

This was Ernest Hemingway's famed tipple. It can be sweetened with half a measure of sugar syrup (see page 122) and downscaled to two measures of rum, if desired.

Put the crushed ice into a blender. Add all the remaining ingredients and blend on high speed until smooth. Pour into a highball glass. Decorate with a grapefruit wedge and serve with straws.

BAHAMAS PUNCH

- juice of 1 lemon
- 1 teaspoon sugar syrup (see page 122)
- 3 drops Angostura bitters
- ½ teaspoon grenadine
- 3 measures golden or white rum
- orange and lemon slices
- ice cubes, cracked
- grated nutmeg, to decorate

Pour the lemon juice and sugar syrup into a mixing glass. Shake in the bitters, then add the grenadine, rum and fruit. Stir and chill. To serve, fill a rocks glass with cracked ice, pour in the punch without straining and sprinkle with grated nutmeg.

HURRICANE

- ice cubes
- 1 measure white rum
- 1 measure gold rum
- 2 teaspoons passion fruit syrup
- 2 teaspoons fresh lime juice

Rum has also been called by various other names, including Barbados Water, Red Eye, Devil's Death and Nelson's Blood – the last because it was believed that Admiral Nelson's body was carried back to England in a barrel of rum.

Put some ice cubes into a cocktail shaker and pour over the rums, passion fruit syrup and lime juice. Shake well. Strain the drink into a Martini glass and add ice cubes.

COOPER COOLER

- 3–4 ice cubes
- 2 measures golden rum
- 3 measures dry ginger ale
- 1 tablespoon fresh lime or lemon juice
- lime or lemon slice, to decorate

Put the ice cubes into a highball glass. Pour over the rum, dry ginger ale and lime or lemon juice and stir. Decorate with lime or lemon slices.

BOLERO

- ice cubes
- 1½ measures white rum
- ¾ measure apple brandy
- several drops sweet vermouth
- lemon rind twist, to decorate

This cocktail uses sweet vermouth. Vermouth, available in sweet and dry types, is a fortified wine with various herbs, barks and roots added as flavourings.

Put some ice into a cocktail shaker and pour over the rum, apple brandy and vermouth. Shake well. Strain into a glass and add ice cubes. Squeeze a lemon rind twist over the glass and drop it in.

FLORIDA SKIES

- ice cubes, cracked
- 1 measure white rum
- ¼ measure fresh lime juice
- ½ measure pineapple juice
- soda water, to top up
- cucumber or lime slices, to decorate

Put some cracked ice into a tall glass. Put the rum and fruit juices into a cocktail shaker. Shake lightly. Strain into the glass and top up with soda water. Decorate with cucumber or lime slices.

ST AUGUSTINE

- ice cubes
- 1½ measures white rum
- 1 measure grapefruit juice
- 1 teaspoon Cointreau
- caster sugar
- lemon rind twist, to decorate

First sold in France in 1875, Cointreau is a clear liqueur flavoured with sweet and bitter oranges.

Put some ice cubes into a cocktail shaker and pour over the rum, grapefruit juice and Cointreau. Shake well. Frost the rim of a glass by dipping into water, then pressing into the sugar. Strain the drink into the prepared glass. Add ice cubes and a lemon rind twist.

RUM OLD-FASHIONED (Pictured)

- 3 ice cubes
- 1 dash Angostura bitters
- 1 dash lime bitters
- 1 teaspoon caster sugar
- ½ measure water
- 2 measures white rum
- ½ measure dark rum
- lime rind twist, to decorate

Stir 1 ice cube with the bitters, sugar and water in a heavy-based rocks glass until the sugar has dissolved. Add the white rum, stir and add the remaining ice cubes. Add the dark rum and stir once again. Decorate with a lime rind twist.

BEAUTIFUL BETH

- 3–4 ice cubes, crushed
- 1 measure light rum
- 1 measure Malibu
- ½ measure Cointreau
- chilled cola, to top up
- cocktail cherries,
  to decorate

Flavoured with natural coconut extract, Malibu is a popular Caribbean rum. It is colourless and has a distinct coconut flavour.

Put the ice cubes into a cocktail shaker. Pour the rum, Malibu and Cointreau over the ice and shake until a frost forms. Strain into a rocks glass and top up with chilled cola. Decorate with cocktail cherries impaled on a cocktail stick.

PINK TREASURE

- 2 ice cubes, cracked
- 1 measure white rum
- 1 measure cherry brandy
- bitter lemon or soda water,
  to taste (optional)
- lemon rind spiral,
  to decorate

Put the cracked ice, rum and cherry brandy into a glass. Add a splash of bitter lemon or soda water, if using. Decorate with a lemon rind spiral.

RUM CRUSTA (Pictured)

- lime wedge
- caster sugar
- crushed ice
- ice cubes
- 2 measures dark rum
- 1 measure Cointreau
- 2 teaspoons maraschino
  liqueur
- 2 teaspoons fresh lime juice
- grape kebab, to decorate

As well as brandy, a Crusta can be made with gin, rum or whisky. This one combines the rich flavour of dark rum with the zesty tang of Cointreau.

Moisten the rim of a rocks glass with the lime wedge and frost with the sugar (see page 144). Fill the glass with crushed ice and half-fill a cocktail shaker with ice cubes. Add all the remaining ingredients to the shaker and shake until a frost forms on the outside of the shaker. Strain over the ice in the glass. Decorate with a grape kebab and serve.

SPICED SIDECAR

- ice cubes
- juice of ½ lemon
- 1 measure Morgan Spiced Rum
- 1 measure brandy
- 1 measure Cointreau
- lemon and orange rind twists, to decorate

Half-fill a cocktail shaker with ice cubes and fill a rocks glass with ice cubes. Add all the remaining ingredients to the shaker and shake until a frost forms on the outside of the shaker. Strain over the ice in the glass. Decorate with lemon and orange rind.

PIÑA COLADA (Pictured)

- 1 scoop crushed ice
- 2 measures white rum
- 2 teaspoons fresh lime juice
- 2 measures coconut cream
- 2 measures pineapple juice
- 1 scoop vanilla ice cream
- pineapple leaf, to decorate

This world-famous cocktail was created by a bartender in Puerto Rico in 1957. It is a homage to the exotic flavours of the country.

Put the crushed ice into a blender. Add all the remaining ingredients and blend on high speed for 20–30 seconds. Pour into a highball glass, decorate with a pineapple leaf and serve.

BLUE HAWAIIAN

- 1 scoop crushed ice
- 1 measure white rum
- ½ measure blue Curaçao
- 2 measures pineapple juice
- 1 measure coconut cream
- pineapple wedge,
  to decorate

Put the crushed ice into a blender. Add all the remaining ingredients and blend on high speed for 20–30 seconds. Pour into a chilled Martini glass. Decorate with a pineapple wedge and serve.

ALMOND CIGAR

- 2 measures golden rum, such as Havana Club 3-year-old
- 1 measure lime cordial
- 1 measure Amaretto di Saronno
- cinnamon stick and lime rind twist, to decorate

This award-winning cocktail was invented by one of the owners of Bugsy's in Prague, Czech Republic, a bar famed throughout Eastern Europe.

Put all the ingredients into a chilled cocktail shaker and shake well. Pour into a chilled Martini glass. Decorate with a cinnamon stick and lime rind twist and serve.

BERLIN BLONDE

- ice cubes
- 1 measure dark rum
- 1 measure Cointreau
- 1 measure double cream
- ground cinnamon,
  to decorate

Half-fill a cocktail shaker with ice cubes. Add all the remaining ingredients and shake until a frost forms on the outside of the shaker. Fine or double strain (see page 66) into a chilled Martini glass. Decorate with a sprinkling of cinnamon and serve.

TOOLS OF THE TRADE

There are all kinds of fancy gizmos and gadgets available for the would-be mixologist but, unless you are planning on hosting cocktail parties on a regular basis, there are just a few must-have items.

COCKTAIL SHAKER

The centrepiece of the bartender's art, this is the one piece of equipment you can't do without. There are two kinds: the Boston Shaker and the European Shaker.

The Boston Shaker is the professional bartender's choice and comes in two parts – a sturdy conical glass and a shaking tin. The ice and all the other ingredients are poured into the tin and then the two parts are pushed together to form a sealed unit before shaking.

The European, or traditional, shaker is the one you are most likely to find on sale. This type of shaker is also probably a better bet for the novice mixologist. Usually made of metal, the European shaker consists of three parts – the conical-shaped shaking tin, its top with a built-in strainer and a tightly fitting cap. Simply put all the ingredients for your cocktail – including the ice – in the tin, put the strainer and cap in place and away you go.

STRAINER

No one wants chunks of ice or fruit seeds floating around in their cocktail, so sometimes recipes call for straining to remove these. This needs a steady hand and eye, and involves pouring the cocktail from the shaker into the glass through a strainer. If you're using a Boston shaker, you'll need a separate strainer but the European shaker has one built in. Bartenders

use a hawthorne strainer – a metal disc with a coiled spring around its edge – but an ordinary tea strainer will do the job. Double or fine straining is sometimes recommended in a recipe to remove every trace of puréed fruit or ice fragments. You could buy a bartender's fine strainer for this but, again, your everyday tea strainer will be a perfectly adequate alternative.

BAR SPOON

This is basically a teaspoon with a very long handle so that it can reach right down to the bottom of the tallest glass. A bar spoon usually has a twisted handle which allows you to pour a small amount of liquid to 'sit' on top of a

cocktail. You carefully pour the liquid from the bottle onto the top of the spoon and it makes its way gradually and evenly down and around the long, twisted handle until it reaches the surface of the drink.

MEASURES

Delicious cocktails are all about achieving the right balance of ingredients and you just can't do this without measures or jiggers, as they are sometimes called. They are little metal containers, generally in standard single or double spirit sizes, so that you can measure out exactly the right amount of alcohol.

MUDDLER

This handy little gadget is similar to the pestle part of a pestle and mortar. It's used to used to bruise mint leaves for a Mojito and to crush fruit, herbs and syrups at the bottom of a glass before making the rest of a cocktail. See page 37 for how to use one.

ICE

You really can't have enough of this, so make sure you prepare enough in advance or, easier still, buy a couple of large bags of ready-made ice cubes to store in the freezer.

Some cocktails need crushed or cracked ice. To crush ice, put ice cubes in a strong polythene bag or between two clean tea towels and hit gently with a rolling pin until it is finely broken. You can make cracked ice the same way but, for this, don't break the ice so finely.

DAIQUIRI

- ice cubes, cracked
- juice of 2 limes
- 1 teaspoon sugar syrup (see page 122)
- 3 measures white rum
- lime wheel, to decorate

A refreshing white rum, lime and sugar beverage invented in the early 20th century by Jennings S Cox, an American working in the mines of the Cuban town of Daiquiri.

Put plenty of cracked ice into a cocktail shaker. Add all the remaining ingredients and shake until a frost forms on the outside of the shaker. Strain into a chilled Martini glass. Decorate with a lime wheel and serve.

FROZEN MANGO DAIQUIRI (Pictured)

- crushed ice
- ½ mango, peeled and stoned
- 1 measure fresh lime juice
- 2 measures white rum
- 1 teaspoon icing sugar
- mango slices, to decorate

Put a small scoop of crushed ice into a food processor or blender. Add the mango, lime juice, rum and icing sugar and blend until smooth. Serve in a Martini glass and decorate with mango slices.

MELON DAIQUIRI

- crushed ice
- 2 measures rum
- 2 measures Midori
- 1 measure fresh lime juice
- lime slice, to decorate

A vibrant green in colour, Midori is a sweet melon liqueur which gets its name from the Japanese word for green.

Put some crushed ice into a cocktail shaker. Pour the rum, Midori and lime juice over the ice and shake until a frost forms. Strain into a chilled Martini glass and decorate with a lime slice.

FROZEN PINEAPPLE DAIQUIRI

- crushed ice
- 2½ pineapple slices
- ½ measure fresh lime juice
- 1 measure white rum
- ¼ measure Cointreau
- 1 teaspoon sugar syrup (see page 122)
- pineapple wedge, to decorate

Put some crushed ice into a food processor or blender. Add the pineapple slices, lime juice, rum, Cointreau and sugar syrup and blend until smooth. Pour into a chilled Martini glass and decorate with a pineapple wedge.

BACARDI COCKTAIL

- ice cubes
- 2 measures Bacardi white rum
- ¾ measure fresh lime juice
- ½ measure grenadine
- lime rind spiral, to decorate

In 1936, a New York State Supreme Court ruled it illegal to make this cocktail without using Bacardi rum.

Half-fill a cocktail shaker with ice cubes. Add all the remaining ingredients and shake until a frost forms on the outside of the shaker. Strain into a chilled Martini glass. Decorate with a lime rind spiral and serve.

TELFORD

- 4–5 ice cubes
- 1 measure white rum
- 1 measure dark rum
- ½ measure tequila
- ½ measure Cointreau
- 1 measure apricot brandy
- 1 measure fresh orange juice
- 2–3 drops orange bitters
- 1 dash grenadine
- cocktail cherries, to decorate

Put the ice cubes into a cocktail shaker. Pour the rums, tequila, Cointreau, apricot brandy, orange juice, bitters and grenadine over the ice and shake until a frost forms. Strain into a Martini glass and decorate with cherries.

EL DORADO (Pictured)

- 4–5 ice cubes
- 1 measure white rum
- 1 measure advocaat
- 1 measure white crème de cacao
- 2 teaspoons grated coconut, plus extra to decorate

Advocaat is a Dutch liqueur that's made from brandy, sugar and egg yolks. Here, it blends with rum and crème de cacao for a smooth, creamy cocktail.

Put the ice cubes into a cocktail shaker. Add all the remaining ingredients and shake until a frost forms on the outside of the shaker. Strain into a chilled Martini glass, decorate with a sprinkling of grated coconut and serve.

PORT ANTONIO

- ½ teaspoon grenadine
- 4–5 ice cubes
- 1 measure fresh lime juice
- 3 measures white or golden rum
- lime rind and cocktail cherry, to decorate

Spoon the grenadine into a chilled Martini glass. Put the ice cubes into a mixing glass. Pour the lime juice and rum over the ice and stir vigorously, then strain into the glass. Wrap the lime rind around the cherry, impale them on a cocktail stick and use to decorate the drink.

YELLOW BIRD

- ice cubes
- 1½ measures white rum
- 1 measure fresh lime juice
- ½ measure Galliano
- ½ measure triple sec

Named after Giuseppe Galliano, a Italian hero of the First Italo-Ethiopian War, Galliano is a sweet liqueur flavoured with spices and herbs including vanilla, anise and peppercorns.

Half-fill a cocktail shaker with ice cubes. Add all the remaining ingredients and shake until a frost forms on the outside of the shaker. Strain into a chilled Martini glass and serve.

RUMMY

- 1 ice cube
- ½ measure fresh lime juice
- ¾ measure dry vermouth
- ½ measure grenadine
- 1 measure Jamaican rum

Put the ice cube into a cocktail shaker and pour over the lime juice, vermouth, grenadine and rum. Shake well and strain into a chilled Martini glass.

RED RUM (Pictured)

- small handful of redcurrants
- ½ measure sloe gin
- ice cubes
- 2 measures Bacardi 8-year-old rum
- ½ measure fresh lemon juice
- ½ measure vanilla syrup
- redcurrant string, to decorate

A beautiful purple-red colour, sloe gin is gin infused with ripe sloe berries and mixed with sugar.

Muddle the redcurrants and sloe gin in a cocktail shaker (see page 37). Add the ice cubes with the remaining ingredients and shake well. Double strain (see page 66) into a chilled Martini glass. Decorate with a redcurrant string.

GAUGUIN

- 3 measures crushed ice
- 2 measures white rum
- 2 teaspoons passion fruit syrup
- 2 teaspoons fresh lemon juice
- 1 teaspoon fresh lime juice
- cocktail cherry, to decorate

Put the crushed ice, rum, passion fruit syrup and fruit juices into a food processor or blender and blend at a low speed for 15 seconds. Strain into a glass and add a cherry to decorate.

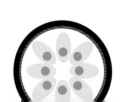

BATISTE (Pictured)

- 4–5 ice cubes
- 1 measure Grand Marnier
- 2 measures golden or dark rum

This cocktail dates back to the 1940s. Add the juice of ½ lime and a twist of lemon peel and it becomes a Prince George, another 1940s cocktail classic.

Put the ice cubes into a mixing glass. Pour the Grand Marnier and rum over the ice, stir vigorously, then strain into a Martini glass.

MAFIA MARTINI

- ice cubes
- 2 measures golden rum
- ½ measure Chambord
- 1 measure apple juice
- lime rind twist, to decorate

Put some ice cubes with the rum, Chambord and apple juice into a cocktail shaker and shake briefly. Double strain (see page 66) into a chilled Martini glass. Decorate with a lime rind twist.

SPICED BERRY

- ice cubes
- 1 measure Morgan Spiced Rum
- 1 dash fresh lime juice
- 1 dash raspberry purée
- 1 dash sugar syrup

Morgan Spiced Rum has a mellow, spicy flavour and is named after 17th-century Welshman, Sir Henry Morgan, a Caribbean pirate.

Put some ice cubes into a cocktail shaker and pour over the rum, lime juice, raspberry purée and sugar syrup. Shake briefly and strain into a chilled shot glass.

RUDE JUDE

- ice cubes
- 1 measure white rum
- 1 dash strawberry purée
- 1 dash strawberry syrup
- 1 dash fresh lime juice

Put some ice cubes into a cocktail shaker and pour over the rum, strawberry purée and syrup and lime juice. Shake well and strain into a shot glass.

GIN

GIN SLING (Pictured)

- 4–5 ice cubes
- juice of ½ lemon
- 1 measure cherry brandy
- 3 measures gin
- soda water, to top up
- maraschino cherry and
  a lemon slice, to decorate

This popular relative of the classic Singapore Sling (see page 80) is a deliciously refreshing long drink with a piquant flavour courtesy of the lemon juice.

Put the ice cubes into a cocktail shaker. Add the lemon juice, cherry brandy and gin and shake until a frost forms on the outside of the shaker. Pour, without straining, into a highball glass and top up with soda water. Decorate with a maraschino cherry and a lemon slice and serve with straws.

THE FIX

- 2 measures gin
- 1 dash pineapple syrup
- 1 dash fresh lime juice
- 1 dash fresh lemon juice
- 1 dash Cointreau
- 6–8 ice cubes
- lemon rind and fresh
  pineapple wedges,
  to decorate

Put the gin, pineapple syrup, fruit juices and Cointreau into a cocktail shaker and shake well. Strain into a rocks glass over the ice cubes and decorate with the lemon rind and the fresh pineapple wedges.

TOM COLLINS

- 2 measures gin
- 1½ teaspoons fresh
  lemon juice
- 1 teaspoon sugar syrup
  (see page 122)
- ice cubes
- soda water, to top up
- lemon wheel, to decorate

This is the best-known of the Collins group of long drinks that first rose to popularity during World War I, originally made with Old Tom, a slightly sweetened gin.

Put the gin, lemon juice and sugar syrup into a highball glass, stir well and fill up with ice cubes. Top up with soda water. Decorate with a lemon wheel and serve.

ZED

- ice cubes, cracked
- 1 measure gin
- 1 measure Mandarine Napoléon
- 3 measures fresh pineapple juice
- 1 teaspoon sugar
- 1 lemon slice, cut in half, and mint sprig to decorate

Put some cracked ice into a cocktail shaker and pour over the gin, Mandarine Napoléon, pineapple juice and sugar. Shake lightly to mix. Pour into a tall glass and decorate with lemon slice halves and mint sprig on top.

SINGAPORE SLING (Pictured)

- ice cubes
- 1 measure gin
- ½ measure cherry brandy
- ¼ measure Cointreau
- ¼ measure Bénédictine
- ½ measure grenadine
- ½ measure fresh lime juice
- 5 measures pineapple juice
- 1 dash Angostura bitters
- pineapple slice and cocktail cherry, to decorate

This legendary cocktail was created by Ngiam Tong Boon, a bartender at the Long Bar in Raffles Hotel, Singapore, around 1915.

Put some ice cubes with all the other ingredients into a cocktail shaker and shake well. Strain over ice cubes in a tall glass. Decorate with a pineapple slice and a cherry.

SALTY DOG

- 2–3 ice cubes
- pinch of salt
- 1 measure gin
- 2–2½ measures fresh grapefruit juice
- orange wheel, to decorate

Put the ice cubes into a rocks glass. Add the salt, pour over the gin and grapefruit juice and stir gently. Decorate with an orange wheel and serve.

PINK GIN

- 1–4 dashes Angostura bitters
- 1 measure gin
- iced water, to top up

Angostura bitters, originally intended for medical use, was added to glasses of gin by the Royal Navy, and thus pink gin was invented.

Shake the bitters into a Martini glass and swirl around to coat the inside of the glass. Add the gin and top up with iced water to taste, then serve.

BRONX

- ice cubes, cracked
- 1 measure gin
- 1 measure sweet vermouth
- 1 measure dry vermouth
- 2 measures fresh orange juice

Put a small glassful of cracked ice into a cocktail shaker. Add all the remaining ingredients, shake briefly to mix and pour into a Martini glass – you can strain the drink if you like.

BURNSIDES

- 8–10 ice cubes
- 2 drops Angostura bitters
- 1 teaspoon cherry brandy
- 1 measure sweet vermouth
- 2 measures dry vermouth
- 2 measures gin
- lemon rind strips,
  to decorate

This cocktail is named after Ambrose Burnside, a Union Army general in the American Civil War. He had distinctive facial hair now known as sideburns, a corruption of his surname.

Put half the ice cubes into a cocktail shaker. Dash the bitters over the ice and add the cherry brandy, vermouths and gin. Shake lightly and strain over the remaining ice cubes in a highball glass. Decorate with lemon rind strips.

CHERRY JULEP (Pictured)

- 3–4 ice cubes, plus finely
  chopped ice to serve
- juice of ½ lemon
- 1 teaspoon sugar syrup
  (see page 122)
- 1 teaspoon grenadine
- 1 measure cherry brandy
- 1 measure sloe gin
- 2 measures gin
- lemon rind strips,
  to decorate

Put the ice cubes into a cocktail shaker. Pour the lemon juice, sugar syrup, grenadine, cherry brandy, sloe gin and gin over the ice. Shake until a frost forms. Strain into a highball glass filled with chopped ice and decorate with lemon rind strips.

RED CLOUD

- ice cubes
- 1½ measures gin
- 2 teaspoons apricot liqueur
- 2 teaspoons fresh lemon
  juice
- 1 teaspoon grenadine
- 1–2 dashes Angostura
  bitters

Reputedly one of the earliest liqueurs ever produced, apricot liqueur is a sweeter, less potent variation on apricot brandy, with additional almond undertones. If you don't have apricot liqueur you can use apricot brandy instead.

Put some ice cubes into a cocktail shaker and pour over the gin, apricot liqueur, lemon juice, grenadine and bitters. Shake well, strain into a glass and add more ice cubes.

HORSE'S NECK

- 4–6 ice cubes
- 1½ measures gin
- dry ginger ale, to top up
- lemon rind spiral,
  to decorate

Put the ice cubes into a tall glass and pour in the gin. Top up with ginger ale, then dangle the lemon rind spiral over the edge of the glass.

TANQSTREAM

- ice cubes, cracked
- 2 measures Tanqueray gin
- 2 teaspoons fresh lime juice
- 3 measures soda water or tonic water
- 2 teaspoons crème de cassis
- lime slices and fresh berries, to decorate

Crème de cassis is a sweet, dark red liqueur made from blackberries. Several cocktails include it, among them the popular Kir which is made up with a measure of crème de cassis topped up with white wine.

Put some cracked ice with the gin and lime juice into a cocktail shaker and shake to mix. Strain into a highball glass half-filled with cracked ice. For a dry Tanqstream, add soda water; for a less dry drink, add tonic water. Stir in the cassis and decorate with the lime slices and fresh berries.

BERRY COLLINS (Pictured)

- 4 raspberries, plus extra to decorate
- 4 blueberries
- 1 dash strawberry syrup
- crushed ice
- 2 measures gin
- 2 teaspoons fresh lemon juice
- sugar syrup (see page 122), to taste
- soda water, to top up

Put the berries and strawberry syrup into a highball glass and muddle together (see page 37). Fill the glass with crushed ice. Pour over the gin, lemon juice and sugar syrup. Stir well and top up with soda water. Decorate with the extra raspberries and serve.

ALBEMARLE FIZZ

- 4–6 ice cubes
- 1 measure Tanqueray gin
- juice of ½ lemon
- 2 dashes raspberry syrup
- ½ teaspoon sugar syrup (see page 122)
- soda water, to top up
- cocktail cherries, to decorate

Tanqueray gin was originally distilled in 1830 by Charles Tanqueray in London. It is renowned for its distinctively smooth, lingering taste.

Put half the ice cubes into a mixing glass and add the gin, lemon juice, raspberry and sugar syrups. Stir to mix, then strain into a highball glass. Add the remaining ice cubes and top up with soda water. Decorate with two cherries impaled on a cocktail stick and serve with straws.

SWEET SIXTEEN

- 6–8 ice cubes
- 2 measures gin
- juice of ½ lime
- 2 dashes grenadine
- 1 teaspoon sugar syrup
  (see page 122)
- bitter lemon, to top up
- lemon rind strip,
  to decorate

Put half the ice cubes into a cocktail shaker and pour over the gin, lime juice, grenadine and sugar syrup. Shake until a frost forms. Put the remaining ice cubes into a highball glass, strain the cocktail over the ice and top up with bitter lemon. Decorate with a lemon rind strip.

GIN FLORADORA

- 4–5 ice cubes
- ½ teaspoon sugar syrup (see page 122)
- juice of ½ lime
- ½ teaspoon grenadine
- 2 measures gin
- dry ginger ale, to top up
- lime rind twist, to decorate

The Floradora takes its name from a musical comedy which was one of the first successful Broadway musicals of the 20th century, and famous for its chorus line of 'Floradora Girls'.

Put the ice cubes into a cocktail shaker. Pour the sugar syrup, lime juice, grenadine and gin over the ice and shake until a frost forms. Pour without straining into a hurricane glass. Top up with dry ginger ale and decorate with a lime rind twist.

ALICE SPRINGS

- 4–5 ice cubes
- 1 measure fresh lemon juice
- 1 measure fresh orange juice
- ½ teaspoon grenadine
- 3 measures gin
- 3 drops Angostura bitters
- soda water, to top up
- orange slice, to decorate

Put the ice cubes into a cocktail shaker. Pour the fruit juices, grenadine and gin over the ice. Add the bitters and shake until a frost forms. Pour into a tall glass and top up with soda water. Decorate with an orange slice and serve with straws.

COLLINSON

- 3 ice cubes, cracked
- 1 dash orange bitters
- 1 measure gin
- ½ measure dry vermouth
- ¼ measure kirsch
- lemon rind
- ½ strawberry and lemon slice, to decorate

This recipes uses kirsch, which is an unsweetened clear liqueur distilled from morello cherries and cherry stones.

Put the cracked ice into a mixing glass, then add the bitters, gin, vermouth and kirsch. Stir well and strain into a Martini glass. Squeeze the zest from the lemon rindover the surface of the cocktail, and decorate the rim of the glass with the strawberry half and lemon slice.

ABBEY ROAD (Pictured)

- 6 mint leaves
- 1 piece candied ginger
- ½ measure fresh lemon juice
- 2 measures gin
- 1 measure apple juice
- ice cubes, plus crushed ice to serve
- lemon wedge, to decorate

Muddle the mint leaves, ginger and lemon juice in a cocktail shaker (see page 37). Add the gin, apple juice and some ice cubes and shake well. Strain over crushed ice in a rocks glass and decorate with a lemon wedge.

NEGRONI

- ice cubes
- 1 measure Plymouth Gin
- 1 measure Campari
- 1 measure red vermouth
- soda water, to top up (optional)
- orange slice, to decorate

An American GI called Negroni stationed in Italy during World War II wanted an extra kick to his Americano cocktail, so the bartender added gin and this cocktail was born.

Put some ice cubes into a mixing glass and fill a rocks glass with ice cubes. Add the gin, Campari and vermouth to the mixing glass, stir briefly to mix and strain over the ice in the glass. Top up with soda water, if you like. Decorate with an orange slice and serve.

MOON RIVER

- 4–5 ice cubes
- ½ measure dry gin
- ½ measure apricot brandy
- ½ measure Cointreau
- ¼ measure Galliano
- ¼ measure fresh lemon juice
- cocktail cherry, to decorate

Put some ice cubes into a mixing glass. Pour the gin, apricot brandy, Cointreau, Galliano and lemon juice over the ice, stir then strain into a large chilled Martini glass. Decorate with a cherry.

ORANGE BLOSSOM

- 2–3 ice cubes
- 1 measure gin
- 1 measure sweet vermouth
- 1 measure fresh orange juice
- orange wheel, to decorate

This is a cocktail from American Prohibition years, when it was sometimes known as an Adirondack.

Put the ice cubes into a highball glass. Put all the remaining ingredients into a chilled cocktail shaker and shake briefly to mix. Pour over the ice in the glass. Decorate with an orange wheel and serve.

HONG KONG SLING (Pictured)

- ice cubes
- 1½ measures gin
- ½ measure lychee liqueur
- 1 measure lychee purée
- 1 measure fresh lemon juice
- ½ measure sugar syrup
  (see page 122)
- soda water, to top up
- fresh lychee in its shell,
  to decorate

Put some ice cubes into a cocktail shaker. Pour over the gin, lychee liqueur and purée, lemon juice and syrup and shake well. Strain over ice into a tall glass. Stir and top up with soda water. Serve with long straws and a lychee.

OPERA

- 4–5 ice cubes
- 1 measure red Dubonnet
- ½ measure orange
  Curaçao
- 2 measures gin
- orange rind spiral,
  to decorate

Dubonnet contains a small amount of quinine and was concocted as a way of making quinine, which combats malaria but has a bitter taste, palatable for French Foreign Legionnaires in North Africa.

Put the ice cubes into a mixing glass. Pour over all the remaining ingredients, stir evenly and strain into a chilled Martini glass. Decorate with an orange rind spiral and serve.

LUIGI (Pictured)

- 4–5 ice cubes
- 1 measure fresh orange
  juice
- 1 measure dry vermouth
- ½ measure Cointreau
- 1 measure grenadine
- 2 measures gin
- orange rind knot,
  to decorate

Put the ice cubes into a mixing glass. Add all the remaining ingredients, stir vigorously and strain into a chilled Martini glass. Decorate with an orange rind knot and serve.

GIN FIZZ

- ice cubes
- 2 measures Plymouth Gin
- 1 measure fresh lemon juice
- 2–3 dashes sugar syrup
  (see page 122)
- ¼ egg white, beaten
- soda water, to top up
- lemon wheels and mint
  sprig, to decorate

Created in the mid-19th century, fizzes are long, gently sparkling drinks, traditionally made with a spirit, lemon juice and sugar, and topped up with a fizzy drink.

Half-fill a cocktail shaker with ice cubes. Add the gin, lemon juice, sugar syrup and egg white and shake briefly to mix. Strain into a highball glass and top up with soda water. Decorate with lemon wheels and a mint sprig and serve.

SAPPHIRE MARTINI

- 4 ice cubes
- 2 measures gin
- ½ measure blue Curaçao
- red or blue cocktail cherry,
  to decorate

Put the ice cubes into a cocktail shaker. Pour in the gin and blue Curaçao. Shake well to mix. Strain into a Martini glass and carefully drop in a cherry.

CLOVER CLUB (Pictured)

- 4–5 ice cubes
- juice of 1 lime
- ½ teaspoon sugar syrup (see page 122)
- 1 egg white
- 3 measures gin
- lime rind, to decorate

This cocktail came into being at the bar of Bellevue-Stratford hotel in Philadelphia, the meeting place of a group of men called The Clover Club, from which the cocktail takes its name.

Put the ice cubes into a cocktail shaker. Add all the remaining ingredients and shake until a frost forms on the outside of the shaker. Strain the cocktail into a highball glass. Decorate with lime rind and serve.

GIN TROPICAL

- 4–6 ice cubes
- 1½ measures gin
- 1 measure fresh lemon juice
- 1 measure passion fruit juice
- ½ measure fresh orange juice
- soda water, to top up
- orange rind spiral, to decorate

Put half the ice cubes into a cocktail shaker and put the remaining half into a rocks glass. Add the gin, lemon juice, passion fruit juice and orange juice to the shaker and shake until a frost forms on the outside of the shaker. Strain over the ice in the glass. Top up with soda water and stir gently. Decorate with an orange rind spiral and serve.

PINK CLOVER CLUB

- 4–5 ice cubes
- juice of 1 lime
- 1 dash grenadine
- 1 egg white
- 3 measures gin
- strawberry slice, to decorate

In this variation a splash of grenadine turns the classic Clover Club, created in about 1911, a pretty pale pink colour.

Put the ice cubes into a cocktail shaker. Pour the lime juice, grenadine, egg white and gin over the ice. Shake until a frost forms, then strain into a Martini glass. Decorate with a strawberry slice and serve with a straw.

GIN CUP

- 3 mint sprigs, plus extra to decorate
- 1 teaspoon sugar syrup (see page 122)
- ice cubes, cracked
- juice of ½ lemon
- 3 measures gin

Put the mint and sugar syrup into a rocks glass and muddle together (see page 37). Fill the glass with cracked ice, add the lemon juice and gin and stir until a frost begins to form on the outside of the glass. Decorate with extra mint sprigs and serve.

VESPER

- ice cubes
- 3 measures gin
- 1 measure vodka
- ½ measure Lillet Blanc
- lemon rind twist,
  to decorate

A Vesper is the version of Martini that James Bond famously orders in the novel *Casino Royale*.

Half-fill a cocktail shaker with ice cubes. Add the gin, vodka and Lillet and shake until a frost forms on the outside of the shaker. Strain into a chilled Martini glass. Decorate with a lemon rind twist and serve.

GINGER TOM

- ice cubes
- 1½ measures gin
- 1 measure Cointreau
- 1 dash fresh lime juice
- 1 dash sweetened ginger
  syrup
- 1½ measures cranberry
  juice
- lime rind spiral, to decorate

Half-fill a cocktail shaker with ice cubes. Add all the remaining ingredients and shake briefly to mix. Strain into a chilled Martini glass. Decorate with a lime rind spiral and serve.

GIMLET

- 2 measures gin
- 1 measure lime cordial
- ice cubes
- ½ measure water
- lime wedge, to decorate

One theory is that this drink is named after British Navy Surgeon General Sir Thomas Gimlette who introduced the drink as a way of getting Navy crew to drink lime juice as protection against scurvy.

Put the gin and lime cordial into a mixing glass, fill up with ice cubes and stir well. Strain into a chilled Martini glass, add the water, then squeeze the lime wedge into the cocktail before adding it to the drink.

MBOLERO (Pictured)

- 2 lime wedges
- ice cubes
- 2 measures gin
- 6 mint leaves
- 6 drops orange bitters
- 1 dash sugar syrup
  (see page 122)
- mint sprig, to decorate

Squeeze the lime wedges into a cocktail shaker. Half-fill the shaker with ice cubes. Add all the remaining ingredients and shake until a frost forms on the outside of the shaker. Fine or double strain (see page 66) into a chilled Martini glass, decorate with a mint sprig and serve.

SMOKY (Pictured)

- ice cubes
- ¼ measure dry vermouth
- 2 measures gin
- 1 measure sloe gin
- 5 drops orange bitters
- orange rind, to decorate

A measure of sloe gin adds an interesting extra dimension to a traditional Martini to create this colourful cocktail.

Put some ice cubes into a mixing glass. Pour over the vermouth and stir until the ice cubes are well coated. Add all the remaining ingredients, stir well and strain into a chilled Martini glass. Decorate with orange rind and serve.

OPAL MARTINI

- ice cubes
- 2 measures gin
- 1 measure Cointreau
- 2 measures fresh orange juice
- orange rind twist, to decorate

Half-fill a cocktail shaker with ice cubes. Add all the remaining ingredients and shake until a frost forms on the outside of the shaker. Strain into a chilled Martini glass. Drape a long twist of orange rind in the drink and around the stem of the glass in a swirl, then serve.

FRENCH '75

- ice cubes, cracked
- 1 measure gin
- juice of ½ lemon
- 1 teaspoon caster sugar
- chilled Champagne or sparkling dry white wine, to top up
- orange wheel, to decorate

Created in 1915 at Harry's New York Bar in Paris, this cocktail was said to have a kick like being shelled by a French 75-mm field gun.

Half-fill a highball glass with cracked ice. Add the gin, lemon juice and sugar and stir well. Top up with chilled Champagne or sparkling dry white wine. Decorate with an orange wheel and serve.

FRENCH '66

- 1 white sugar cube
- 6 dashes orange bitters
- 1 measure sloe gin
- juice of ¼ lemon
- chilled Champagne,
  to top up
- lemon rind spiral,
  to decorate

Soak the sugar in the bitters, then drop it into a Champagne flute. Add the sloe gin and lemon juice and stir. Top up with chilled Champagne. Decorate with a lemon rind spiral and serve.

AVIATION (Pictured)

- ice cubes
- 2 measures gin
- ½ measure maraschino liqueur
- ½ measure fresh lemon juice
- maraschino cherry, to decorate

Maraschino cherries are preserved in alcohol and then soaked in sugar and food colourings to give them their distinctive flavour. They're an essential store cupboard item for budding mixologists.

Half-fill a cocktail shaker with ice cubes. Add all the remaining ingredients and shake until a frost forms on the outside of the shaker. Fine or double strain (see page 66) into a chilled Martini glass. Decorate with a maraschino cherry and serve.

DELFT DONKEY

- 3–4 ice cubes, cracked
- 2 measures gin
- juice of 1 lemon
- ginger beer, to top up
- lemon slice, to decorate

Put the cracked ice into a cocktail shaker and pour over the gin and lemon juice. Shake until a frost forms. Pour into a hurricane or other large glass. Top up with ginger beer. Decorate with a lemon slice and serve with a straw.

GIBSON

- 5–6 ice cubes
- ½ measure dry vermouth
- 3 measures gin
- cocktail onion, to decorate

The Martini purist mixes their tipple with an almost religious fervour. So if you prefer a cocktail onion in your drink rather than an olive, it's a Gibson, not a Martini.

Put the ice cubes into a mixing glass. Pour over the vermouth and gin and stir (never shake) vigorously and evenly without splashing. Strain into a chilled Martini glass. Decorate with a cocktail onion and serve.

MAIDEN'S BLUSH

- ice cubes
- 2 measures gin
- 1 measure Pernod
- 1 teaspoon grenadine

Put some ice cubes into a cocktail shaker and pour over the gin, Pernod and grenadine. Shake well and strain into a Martini glass.

THE GLASS IS ALWAYS HALF-FULL

Most people have a set of wine glasses, some mismatched tumblers and maybe a set of Champagne flutes in the cupboard. While this is fine for everyday use, it won't do when it comes to serving cocktails. As already mentioned, a cocktail needs to look fantastic and handing over a beautifully crafted Moscow Mule in a wine glass you got free from the petrol station is a real faux pas. These illustrious drinks require superior vessels and you simply must invest in new glassware before you start measuring out the spirits. Of course, it's easy to get carried away, so we'll go through the glasses in order of importance, with the ones listed last being reserved for those with extra-large cupboards and serious intentions.

HIGHBALL GLASS

This is the Jack-of-all-trades of glassware, as it can be used for straight mixer drinks, such as Vodka and Tonic, as well as any long cocktail.

CHAMPAGNE FLUTE

The long, elegant lines help to keep the bubbles intact in sparkling drinks, hence their natural partnership with Champagne.

ROCKS

Also called an old-fashioned glass, this sturdy tumbler-style glass is ideal for straight spirits and muddled drinks, like the Mojito or Caipirinha.

SHOT GLASS

These are used for quick-hit drinks, which can be simple single or double servings of spirits and carefully layered creations, such as the B-52.

MARTINI GLASS

This is the classic cocktail glass and it's used for so much more than just Martinis so it won't sit in the back of the cupboard gathering dust. With its distinctive triangular shape and delicate stem, it's sophisticated enough to play host to the most extravagant drink in your repertoire.

HURRICANE

Not seen much these days, apart from in the beach bars of holiday resorts, this is called a hurricane glass because it is the same shape as a hurricane lamp. A hurricane glass is usually used to serve long, creamy cocktails.

MARGARITA

If you know you'll be serving Margaritas then it's worth investing in a few glasses to show the drinks off at their best. You can also use these for Daiquiris and other drinks with fruit garnishes.

BALLOON

If you're having the kind of cocktail party where elders in tweed kick back by the fire cradling a Scotch, then move these further up the list. If not, then you can probably survive without them.

GIN GARDEN (Pictured)

- ¼ cucumber, peeled and chopped, plus extra peeled slices to decorate
- ½ measure elderflower cordial
- ice cubes
- 2 measures gin
- 1 measure pressed apple juice

Elderflower cordial is non-alcoholic and is made with the flowers of the elderberry. Recipes for the cordial can be traced back to Roman times.

Put the cucumber and elderflower cordial into a cocktail shaker and muddle together (see page 37). Half-fill the shaker with ice cubes. Add the gin and apple juice and shake until a frost forms on the outside of the shaker. Fine or double strain (see page 66) into a chilled Martini glass. Decorate with peeled cucumber slices and serve.

FAIR LADY

- lightly beaten egg white
- caster sugar
- ice cubes
- 1 measure gin
- 4 measures grapefruit juice
- 1 dash Cointreau

Frost the rim of a rocks glass by dipping into egg white and pressing into sugar (see page 144). Put some ice cubes into a cocktail shaker and pour over the remaining egg white, gin, grapefruit juice and Cointreau. Shake well, then pour into the prepared glass.

ZAZA

- 5–6 ice cubes
- 3 drops orange bitters
- 1 measure Dubonnet
- 2 measures gin

Named after its creator Joseph Dubonnet, Dubonnet is a sweet fortified wine blended with various herbs and spices. A Dubonnet and gin is reputed to have been a favourite tipple of the Queen Mother.

Put the ice cubes into a mixing glass. Shake the bitters over the ice, pour in the Dubonnet and gin and stir vigorously without splashing. Strain into a chilled Martini glass.

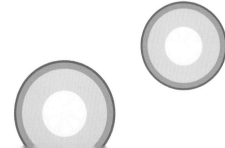

TURF

- ice cubes
- 1 measure gin
- 1 measure dry vermouth
- 1 teaspoon fresh lemon juice
- 1 teaspoon Pernod
- lemon slice, to decorate

Put some ice cubes into a cocktail shaker and pour over gin, vermouth, lemon juice and Pernod. Shake well, then strain into a glass containing more ice. Decorate with a lemon slice.

CROSSBOW

- drinking chocolate powder
- 4–5 ice cubes
- ½ measure gin
- ½ measure crème de cacao
- ½ measure Cointreau

Perfect for chocoholics, this cocktail combines crème de cacao which is a clear, chocolate-flavoured liqueur with the orange flavour of Cointreau.

Frost the rim of a chilled Martini glass by dipping into a little water and pressing into drinking chocolate powder (see page 144). Put the ice cubes into a cocktail shaker and add the gin, crème de cacao and Cointreau. Shake vigorously and strain into the prepared glass.

PARK LANE SPECIAL

- ice cubes
- 2 measures gin
- ½ measure apricot brandy
- ½ measure fresh orange juice
- 1 dash grenadine
- ½ egg white

Put some ice cubes into a cocktail shaker and pour over the remaining ingredients. Shake well and strain into a Martini glass.

PARADISE (Pictured)

- 3 ice cubes, cracked
- 1 dash fresh lemon juice
- ½ measure fresh orange juice
- 1 measure gin
- ½ measure apricot brandy
- orange and lemon slices, to decorate

The first printed recipe of this, one of the less well-known classic cocktails, was written by Harry Craddock, the famous barman who worked at the American Bar at the Savoy Hotel, London from 1920.

Put the cracked ice into a cocktail shaker. Pour over the fruit juices, gin and apricot brandy and shake well. Strain into a chilled Martini glass and decorate with orange and lemon slices.

HONOLULU

- 4–5 ice cubes
- 1 measure pineapple juice
- 1 measure fresh lemon juice
- 1 measure fresh orange juice
- ½ teaspoon grenadine
- 3 measures gin
- pineapple slice and cocktail cherry, to decorate

Put the ice cubes into a cocktail shaker and pour over the fruit juices, grenadine and gin. Shake until a frost forms. Strain into a chilled Martini glass and decorate with a pineapple slice and a cherry.

JULIANA BLUE

- crushed ice, plus 2–3 ice cubes
- 1 measure gin
- ½ measure Cointreau
- ½ measure blue Curaçao
- 2 measures pineapple juice
- ½ measure fresh lime juice
- 1 measure coconut cream
- pineapple slice and cocktail cherries, to decorate

Curaçao is made from the dried peel of the laraha citrus fruit grown on the Caribbean island of Curaçao. It is naturally colourless but is usually coloured either blue or orange.

Put some crushed ice into a food processor or blender and pour in the gin, Cointreau, blue Curaçao, fruit juices and coconut cream. Blend at high speed for several seconds until the mixture has the consistency of soft snow. Strain over ice cubes in a Martini glass. Decorate with a pineapple slice and cherries.

PERFECT LADY

- ice cubes
- 2 measures gin
- 1 measure peach brandy
- 1 measure fresh lemon juice
- 1 dash egg white

Fill a mixing glass three-quarters full with ice cubes. Add the gin, peach brandy, lemon juice and egg white and stir well. Strain into a chilled Martini glass.

CLASSIC DRY MARTINI (Pictured)

- ½ measure dry vermouth
- 3 measures ice-cold gin
- green olive or lemon rind twist, to decorate

This most famous cocktail of all was invented at the Knickerbocker Hotel in New York in 1910.

Swirl the vermouth around the inside of a chilled Martini glass, then discard the excess. Pour in the ice-cold gin and add an olive or lemon rind twist.

VAMPIRE

- 1 measure dry vermouth
- 1 measure gin
- ½ measure fresh lime juice

Put all the ingredients into a cocktail shaker and shake well. Pour into a chilled Martini glass.

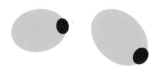

WHITE LADY (Pictured)

- 1 measure gin
- 1 measure Cointreau
- 1 measure fresh lemon juice
- lemon rind twist,
  to decorate

This classic cocktail is also known as a Delilah, Chelsea Sidecar or Lillian Forever.

Pour the gin, Cointreau and lemon juice into a cocktail shaker. Shake well, strain into a chilled Martini glass and decorate with a lemon rind twist.

SLOE GIN SLING

- 1 measure sloe gin
- ½ measure fresh lemon juice
- soda water, to top up
- lemon or orange slice, to decorate
- mint sprig, to decorate

Pour the sloe gin and lemon juice into a highball glass. Top up with soda water. Decorate with a lemon or orange slice and a mint sprig.

PAPA'S FLIGHT

- ice cubes
- 2 measures gin
- 2 teaspoons maraschino liqueur
- 1 measure grapefruit juice
- 1 dash fresh lime juice
- 1 dash sugar syrup
- orange rind, to decorate

Maraschino liqueur is made with marasca cherries and has a faint almond flavour which comes from the crushed pits of the cherries that are also used in its manufacture.

Put some ice cubes with the gin, maraschino, fruit juices and sugar syrup into a cocktail shaker and shake to mix. Strain into a chilled Martini glass and decorate with orange rind.

SAN FRANCISCO

- ice cubes
- 1½ measures sloe gin
- ¼ measure sweet vermouth
- ¼ measure dry vermouth
- 1 dash orange bitters
- 1 dash Angostura bitters
- cocktail cherry, to decorate

Put some ice cubes into a mixing glass. Add the gin, vermouths and bitters and stir well. Pour into a Martini glass and decorate with a cherry.

WHISKY

MISSISSIPPI PUNCH

- crushed ice
- 3 drops Angostura bitters
- 1 teaspoon sugar syrup
- juice of 1 lemon
- 1 measure brandy
- 1 measure dark rum
- 2 measures bourbon whiskey

Bourbon whiskey is an American whiskey which gets its name from an area of Bourbon County in Kentucky.

Half-fill a tall glass with crushed ice. Shake the bitters over the ice. Pour in the sugar syrup and the lemon juice, then stir gently to mix thoroughly. Add the brandy, rum and bourbon, in that order, stir once and serve with straws.

BENEDICT (Pictured)

- 3–4 ice cubes
- 1 measure Bénédictine
- 3 measures whisky
- dry ginger ale, to top up

Put the ice cubes into a mixing glass. Pour the Bénédictine and whisky over the ice. Stir evenly without splashing. Pour without straining into a chilled highball glass. Top up with dry ginger ale.

RHETT BUTLER

- 4–5 ice cubes, plus extra to serve
- 2 measures bourbon whiskey
- 4 measures cranberry juice
- 2 tablespoons sugar syrup (see page 122)
- 1 tablespoon fresh lime juice
- lime slices, to decorate

This bourbon-based cocktail is named after the famous character portrayed by Clark Gable in *Gone with the Wind*.

Put the ice cubes with the bourbon, cranberry juice, sugar syrup and lime juice into a cocktail shaker and shake well. Fill a rocks glass with ice cubes and strain the cocktail over them. Decorate with lime slices and serve with straws.

CAPRICORN

- 4–5 ice cubes, cracked
- 1 measure bourbon whiskey
- ½ measure apricot brandy
- ½ measure fresh lemon juice
- 2 measures orange juice
- orange slice, to decorate

Put half the cracked ice cubes into a cocktail shaker and add the whiskey, apricot brandy and the lemon and orange juices. Shake to mix. Put the remaining ice into a rocks glass and strain the cocktail over them. Decorate with an orange slice.

MINT JULEP

- 10 mint leaves, plus an extra sprig to decorate
- 1 teaspoon sugar syrup (see page 122)
- 4 dashes Angostura bitters
- crushed ice
- 2 measures bourbon

This is the ultimate cocktail of America's Deep South. The earliest written reference dates this aperitif back to 1803.

Put the mint leaves, sugar syrup and bitters into a highball glass and muddle together (see page 37). Fill the glass with crushed ice. Pour over the bourbon and stir well. Decorate with a mint sprig and serve.

VIRGINIA MINT JULEP (Pictured)

- 9 young mint sprigs, plus extra to decorate
- 1 teaspoon sugar syrup (see page 122)
- crushed ice
- 3 measures bourbon whiskey

Muddle the mint and sugar syrup (see page 37) in a highball glass. Fill the glass with crushed ice, pour the bourbon over the ice and stir gently. Pack in more crushed ice and stir until a frost forms. Wrap the glass in a table napkin and serve decorated with a mint sprig.

BOBBY BURNS

- 4–5 ice cubes
- 1 measure Scotch whisky
- 1 measure dry vermouth
- 1 tablespoon Bénédictine
- lemon rind spiral, to decorate

Bénédictine is a liqueur made from brandy and over 20 spices and plant extracts. It dates from the 16th century, when it was created by a Bénédictine monk in Normandy, France.

Put the ice cubes into a cocktail shaker. Add all the remaining ingredients and shake until a frost forms on the outside of the shaker. Strain into a chilled Martini glass. Decorate with a lemon rind spiral and serve.

RICKEY

- 4–5 ice cubes
- 1½ measures whisky
- 1½ measures fresh lime juice
- soda water, to top up
- lime rind twist, to decorate

Put the ice cubes into a highball glass. Pour over the whisky and lime juice. Top up with soda water and stir. Decorate with a lime rind twist and serve.

BIG BUFF (Pictured)

- 1 strawberry
- 3 raspberries
- 3 blueberries
- 2 teaspoons Chambord
- ice cubes
- 1 dash fresh lime juice
- 2 measures Buffalo Trace Bourbon Whiskey
- 3 measures cranberry juice

A fruity version of the Rhett Butler (see page 112), containing a mixture of berries. It uses Buffalo Trace Bourbon, which has a delicious vanilla character.

Put the mixed berries and the Chambord into a cocktail shaker and muddle together (see page 37). Half-fill the shaker with ice cubes. Add all the remaining ingredients and shake until a frost forms on the outside of the shaker. Pour, without straining, into a highball glass and serve.

KICKER

- 1 measure whisky
- 1 measure Midori
- ice cubes, to serve (optional)

Combine the whisky and Midori in a mixing glass and serve chilled or on the rocks.

RATTLESNAKE

- 4–5 ice cubes, plus extra to serve
- 1½ measures whisky
- 1 teaspoon fresh lemon juice
- 1 teaspoon sugar syrup (see page 122)
- 1 egg white
- few drops Pernod

This classic cocktail first appeared in the 1930 edition of the *Savoy Cocktail Book*, the bartending manual of the Savoy Hotel in London.

Put all the ingredients into a cocktail shaker and shake extremely well. Strain into a glass and add more ice.

VANILLA DAISY

- crushed ice
- 2 measures bourbon
- 1 measure fresh lemon juice
- 1 measure vanilla syrup
- 1 teaspoon grenadine
- 2 maraschino cherries, to decorate

Put some crushed ice into a cocktail shaker and fill a rocks glass with crushed ice. Add the bourbon, lemon juice and vanilla syrup to the shaker and shake until a frost forms on the outside of the shaker. Strain over the ice in the glass. Drizzle the grenadine through the drink. Decorate with the maraschino cherries and serve.

LYNCHBURG LEMONADE

- ice cubes
- 1½ measures Jack Daniel's
- 1 measure Cointreau
- 1 measure fresh lemon juice
- lemonade, to top up
- lemon slices, to decorate

A classic based on Jack Daniel's 'sour mash' Tennessee whiskey, this cocktail was specially created for the Jack Daniel's distillery in Lynchburg, Tennessee.

Put some ice cubes with the whiskey, Cointreau and lemon juice into a cocktail shaker and shake well. Strain into a highball glass filled with ice cubes. Top up with lemonade and stir. Decorate with lemon slices.

SOUTHERLY BUSTER

- 4–5 ice cubes
- 1 measure blue Curaçao
- 3 measures whisky
- lemon rind strip, to decorate

Put the ice cubes into a mixing glass. Pour the Curaçao and whisky over the ice, stir vigorously, then strain into a chilled Martini glass. Twist the lemon rind strip over the drink and drop it in. Serve with a straw.

RUSTY NAIL

- ice cubes
- 1½ measures Scotch whisky
- 1 measure Drambuie

If served without ice, this classic cocktail is known as a Straight-up Nail.

Fill a rocks glass with ice cubes and pour over the Scotch whisky and Drambuie. Stir gently.

BOURBON PEACH SMASH (Pictured)

- 6 mint leaves
- 3 peach slices
- 3 lemon slices
- 2 teaspoons caster sugar
- ice cubes
- crushed ice
- 2 measures bourbon whiskey
- lemon wedge, to decorate

Put the mint leaves, peach and lemon slices and sugar into a cocktail shaker and muddle together (see page 37). Half-fill the shaker with ice cubes and put some crushed ice into a rocks glass. Add the bourbon to the shaker and shake until a frost forms on the outside of the shaker. Strain over the ice in the glass. Decorate with a lemon wedge and serve.

MANHATTAN

- ice cubes
- 2 measures rye whiskey
  or bourbon
- 1 measure extra dry
  vermouth
- 4 dashes Angostura bitters
- maraschino cherry,
  to decorate

This vintage cocktail was reputedly created at New York's Manhattan Club at the request of Sir Winston Churchill's mother, Lady Randolph Churchill, who was hosting a party for a politician.

Put some ice cubes into a mixing glass. Add all the remaining ingredients and stir. Strain into a chilled Martini glass. Decorate with a maraschino cherry and serve.

ECLIPSE (Pictured)

- ice cubes
- crushed ice
- 2 measures Jack Daniel's
- ½ measure Chambord
- ½ measure fresh lime juice
- 1 dash sugar syrup
  (see page 122)
- 1 measure cranberry juice
- 1 measure raspberry purée
- raspberry and a lime
  wedge, to decorate

Half-fill a cocktail shaker with ice cubes and put some crushed ice into a large highball glass. Add all the remaining ingredients to the shaker and shake until a frost forms on the outside of the shaker. Strain over the ice in the glass. Decorate with a raspberry and a lime wedge and serve with long straws.

OLD-FASHIONED

- 2 measures bourbon
- ice cubes
- 1 teaspoon sugar syrup
  (see page 122)
- 4 dashes Angostura bitters
- orange rind twist,
  to decorate

Short for Old-fashioned Whiskey Cocktail, and with the old-fashioned, or rocks, glass named after it, this is one of those classic cocktails whose authentic recipe is hotly debated.

Pour the bourbon into a rocks glass and add a few ice cubes. Build the sugar syrup and then the bitters over the ice. Decorate with an orange rind twist and serve.

GODFATHER

- ice cubes
- 2 measures J&B Rare
  Scotch whisky
- 1 measure Amaretto di
  Saronno

Put some ice cubes with the whisky and Amaretto into a cocktail shaker and shake vigorously. Strain into a small old-fashioned glass filled with ice cubes.

KEEP YOUR SPIRITS UP

When it's time to stock up your bar you need to think about what you're actually going to use. If you're throwing a cocktail party it's best to choose a select list of cocktails to offer your guests, unless you want to spend a fortune. There are key spirits that are used in many different drinks so work out your menu, then shop accordingly.

MIXING IT UP

Although spirits are the stars of the cocktail world, they would fail to shine if it weren't for the presence of mixers. Stock your store cupboard with cola, lemonade, tonic and a good selection of fruit juices, depending on the recipes you're going to make (orange, apple, grapefruit, cranberry and pineapple are used in a lot of drinks). You'll also need a pile of lemons and limes, both for their juice and their segments. If you're taking your new role of mixologist seriously, then you should also have a batch of sugar syrup, Tabasco sauce and Angostura bitters to hand.

SUGAR SYRUP

This is used to sweeten many cocktails because it blends into a cold drink faster than ordinary sugar and it gives the cocktail body. It is available ready made but it's easy to make your own.

Put 4 tablespoons granulated sugar and 4 tablespoons water into a small saucepan and bring slowly to the boil, stirring to dissolve the sugar. Boil without stirring for 1–2 minutes then leave to cool. Store in a sterilized bottle in the refrigerator for up to 2 months.

RUM

From the kitsch Piña Colada to the refreshing Cuba Libre, rum brings an exotic flavour to any drink. Some cocktails use light rum and others dark, so check the ingredients before you hit the shops.

TEQUILA

The famous Mexican export is probably best known for its use in the Margarita. Not for the faint-hearted, this ancient spirit should definitely be on the mixologist's list.

WHISKY

You can spend a lot of money on a bottle of whisky, so if you're going for top quality, save it for sipping. For cocktails, put your money somewhere in the middle and treat your guests to a Whisky Sour or a classy Manhattan.

BRANDY

Brandy has a strong and distinctive flavour so you won't find it in as many cocktail recipes as other spirits. However, if you like nothing more than relaxing with a Brandy Alexander, then make sure you have a bottle in your bar.

GIN

This is an essential in any bartender's cupboard, as it's used in so many different cocktails. It's no coincidence that probably the most popular and simplest cocktail in the world – the Gin and Tonic – uses this as its main ingredient.

VODKA

Another widely used cocktail spirit, this flavour-free drink is perfect as it can be combined with virtually any mixer, so it's incredibly versatile.

RITZ OLD-FASHIONED (Pictured)

- lightly beaten egg white
- caster sugar
- 3 ice cubes, crushed
- 1½ measures bourbon
- ½ measure Grand Marnier
- 1 dash fresh lemon juice
- 1 dash Angostura bitters
- 2 maraschino cherries
  and an orange rind twist,
  to decorate

The Old-fashioned (see page 120) is given a facelift here with the addition of Grand Marnier and lemon juice. A sugar rim completes the new look.

Moisten the rim of a rocks glass with the egg white and frost with the sugar (see page 144). Put the crushed ice into a cocktail shaker. Add all the remaining ingredients and shake briefly to mix. Strain into the glass. Decorate with 2 maraschino cherries and an orange rind twist and serve.

SILKY PIN

- ice cubes
- 1 measure Scotch whisky
- 1 measure Drambuie

Fill a rocks glass with ice cubes and pour over the whisky and Drambuie. Stir gently.

WHISKY MAC

- 3–4 ice cubes
- 1 measure Scotch whisky
- 1 measure ginger wine

The full name of this warming cocktail is Whisky MacDonald and it is reputed to have been invented by a Colonel MacDonald serving in India at the time of the British Raj.

Put the ice cubes into a rocks glass. Pour over the whisky and ginger wine, stir lightly and serve.

WHISKY SOUR

- ice cubes
- 2 measures whisky
- 1½ measures fresh lemon juice
- 1 egg white
- 2 tablespoons caster sugar
- 4 dashes Angostura bitters
- lemon slice and cocktail cherry, to decorate

Put some ice cubes with the whisky, lemon juice, egg white, sugar and bitters into a shaker and shake well. Strain into a sour glass filled with ice cubes and decorate with a lemon slice and a cherry on a cocktail stick.

HARLEQUIN (Pictured)

- 5 white grapes, halved
- ½ measure sweet vermouth
- 6 dashes orange bitters
- crushed ice
- 2 measures Canadian Club Whisky

Canadian Club Whisky is aged in white oak, giving it a lighter, smoother taste than most Scotches and bourbons. It works particularly well with sweet vermouth in this elegant cocktail.

Put the grapes, vermouth and bitters into a rocks glass. Half-fill the glass with crushed ice and stir well. Add the whisky, top up with crushed ice and serve.

NEW YORKER

- 2–3 ice cubes, cracked
- 1 measure Scotch whisky
- 1 teaspoon fresh lime juice
- 1 teaspoon icing sugar
- finely grated rind of ½ lemon
- lemon rind spiral, to decorate

Put the cracked ice into a cocktail shaker and add the whisky, lime juice and sugar. Shake until a frost forms. Strain into a Martini glass. Sprinkle the grated lemon rind over the surface and decorate the rim with a lemon rind spiral.

IRISH COFFEE

- 1 measure Irish whiskey
- hot filter coffee
- lightly whipped cream
- ground coffee, to decorate

This classic combination was hit upon on an icy winter night in the early 1940s as a way to warm up passengers disembarking from a trans-Atlantic flying boat in Ireland.

Put a bar spoon into a large toddy glass. Add the whiskey, top up with coffee and stir. Heat the cream very slightly and pour into the bowl of the spoon resting on top of the coffee to get a good float. Decorate with a sprinkling of ground coffee and serve.

ABERDEEN ANGUS

- 2 measures Scotch whisky
- 1 measure Drambuie
- 1 teaspoon clear honey
- 2 teaspoons fresh lime juice

Combine the whisky and the honey in a mug and stir until smooth. Add the lime juice. Warm the Drambuie in a small saucepan over a low heat. Pour into a ladle, ignite and pour into the mug. Stir and serve immediately.

WHISKY DAISY

- ice cubes
- 2 measures Scotch whisky or bourbon whiskey
- 1 measure fresh lemon juice
- 1 teaspoon caster sugar
- 1 teaspoon grenadine
- soda water, to top up
- lemon rind spiral, to decorate

Daisies are refreshing, spirit-based drinks dating from the 19th century that include grenadine or a sweet liqueur and lemon or lime juice. The Whisky Daisy is probably the best known.

Put some ice cubes with the whisky, lemon juice, sugar and grenadine in a cocktail shaker and shake well. Strain into a rocks glass filled with ice cubes and top up with soda water, if you like. Decorate with a lemon rind spiral

AMERICAN BELLE

- ½ measure cherry liqueur
- ½ measure Amaretto di Saronno
- ½ measure bourbon whiskey

Pour the cherry liqueur into a shot glass. Using the back of a bar spoon, slowly float the Amaretto over the cherry liqueur (see page 36). Pour the bourbon over the Amaretto in the same way.

NERIDA (Pictured)

- 4–5 ice cubes
- juice of ½ lime or lemon
- 3 measures Scotch whisky
- dry ginger ale, to top up
- lime or lemon wheels, to decorate

A glamorous version of the classic Scotch and Dry, this cocktail relies on the character of the whisky to work its magic.

Put the ice cubes into a cocktail shaker. Add the lime or lemon juice and whisky and shake until a frost forms on the outside of the shaker. Pour, without straining, into a chilled highball glass. Top up with dry ginger ale and stir gently. Decorate with lime or lemon wheels and serve.

SICILIAN KISS

- crushed ice
- 2 measures Southern Comfort
- 1 measure Amaretto di Saronno
- lemon slice, to decorate

Put plenty of crushed ice with the bourbon and Amaretto in a rocks glass and stir to mix. Decorate with a lemon slice.

TEQUILA

TIJUANA SLING (Pictured)

- ice cubes
- 1¼ measures tequila
- ¾ measure crème de cassis
- ¾ measure fresh lime juice
- 2 dashes Peychaud's bitters
- 3½ measures dry ginger ale
- lime slice and blackcurrants or blueberries, to decorate

Created in about 1830 in New Orleans, Peychaud's bitters are similar to Angostura bitters but with a lighter, sweeter taste.

Put some ice cubes with the tequila, crème de cassis, lime juice and bitters into a cocktail shaker and shake vigorously. Pour into a tall glass, then top up with dry ginger ale. Decorate with a lime slice and some berries.

JAPANESE SLIPPER

- 4–5 ice cubes
- 1¼ measures tequila
- ¾ measure Midori
- 1¼ measure fresh lime juice
- lime wheel, to decorate

Put the ice cubes into a cocktail shaker. Add all the remaining ingredients and shake until a frost forms on the outside of the shaker. Strain into a Martini glass. Decorate with a lime wheel and serve.

TEQUILA SUNRISE

- ice cubes
- 2 measures tequila
- 4 measures fresh orange juice
- 2 teaspoons grenadine
- orange slices, to decorate

This classic cocktail from the 1970s gets its name from the gradations in colour it has, created as the grenadine sinks down the glass, which mimic the appearance of the sun rising.

Put some ice cubes with the tequila and orange juice into a cocktail shaker and shake to mix. Strain into a highball glass filled with ice cubes. Slowly pour in the grenadine and allow it to settle. Decorate with an orange slice.

FLORECIENTE

- 1 orange slice
- fine sea salt
- crushed ice
- 1¼ measures tequila gold
- ¾ measure fresh lemon juice
- ¾ measure fresh blood orange juice
- blood orange wedge, to decorate

Frost the rim of a large rocks glass by moistening with an orange slice then pressing the glass into salt (see page 144). Fill it with crushed ice. Pour the tequila, Cointreau, lemon juice and blood orange juice into a cocktail shaker, shake vigorously for 10 seconds, then strain into the prepared glass. Decorate with a blood orange wedge.

BORDER CROSSING

- ice cubes
- 1½ measures gold tequila
- 1 measure fresh lime juice
- 1 measure clear honey
- 4 dashes orange bitters
- 3 measures dry ginger ale
- blueberries and lime wedges, to decorate

Made from Seville oranges, cardamom, caraway seeds and coriander, orange bitters fell out of use around the time of Prohibition but is gaining a new following among 21st-century cocktail drinkers.

Put some ice cubes with the tequila, lime juice, honey and orange bitters in a cocktail shaker and shake well. Pour into a highball glass and top up with the dry ginger ale. Decorate with blueberries and lime wedges.

MEXICAN MULE

- 1 lime
- 1 dash sugar syrup (see page 122)
- crushed ice
- 1 measure José Cuervo Gold tequila
- 1 measure Kahlúa
- dry ginger ale, to top up

Cut the lime into slices, put them into a highball glass and muddle with the sugar syrup (see page 37). Half-fill the glass with crushed ice and add the tequila and Kahlúa. Stir well, then top up with dry ginger ale.

BLOODY MARIA

- pepper
- celery salt
- 1 lime wedge
- ice cubes
- 1¼ measures tequila
- 2 teaspoons medium sherry
- 2 dashes Tabasco sauce
- 4 dashes Worcestershire sauce
- 1 tablespoon fresh lime juice
- 4 measures tomato juice
- cayenne pepper
- celery stick, lime wedge and basil sprig, to decorate

Tequila replaces vodka in this variation of the classic Bloody Mary. The spicy kick combined with tomato juice and alcohol makes it a popular hangover 'cure'.

Mix some pepper and celery salt together on a small saucer. Moisten the rim of a rocks glass with the lime wedge, then frost with the pepper and salt mixture (see page 144). Half-fill a cocktail shaker with ice cubes. Add the tequila, sherry, Tabasco sauce, Worcestershire sauce, lime juice, tomato juice and a pinch each of celery salt, pepper and cayenne pepper. Shake until a frost forms on the outside of the shaker and pour into the glass. Decorate with a celery stick, lime wedge and basil sprig and serve.

AGAVE JULEP (Pictured)

- 8 torn mint leaves
- 1 tablespoon sugar syrup (see page 122)
- 1¼ measures tequila gold
- 1¼ measures fresh lime juice
- crushed ice
- lime wedge and mint sprig, to decorate

Muddle the mint leaves with the sugar syrup (see page 37) in a highball glass. Add the tequila and lime juice, fill the glass with crushed ice and stir vigorously to mix. Decorate with a lime wedge and a mint sprig.

MEXICANA

- 8–10 ice cubes
- 1¼ measures tequila
- ¾ measure framboise liqueur
- ¾ measure fresh lemon juice
- 3½ measures pineapple juice
- pineapple wedge and lemon slice, to decorate

This cocktail uses framboise liqueur, which is a sweet, red, raspberry-flavoured liqueur made in France.

Put half the ice cubes with the tequila, framboise and fruit juices into a cocktail shaker and shake vigorously for about 10 seconds. Pour over the remaining ice cubes in a large highball glass and decorate with a pineapple wedge and a lemon slice.

SILK STOCKING (Pictured)

- cocoa powder
- 4–5 ice cubes
- ¾ measure tequila
- ¾ measure white crème de cacao
- 4 measures single cream
- 2 teaspoons grenadine

Moisten the rim of a chilled Martini glass with water and frost with the cocoa powder (see page 144). Put the ice cubes into a cocktail shaker. Add all the remaining ingredients and shake until a frost forms on the outside of the shaker. Strain into the glass and serve.

MEXICAN BULLDOG

- ice cubes
- ¾ measure tequila
- ¾ measure Kahlúa
- 1¼ measures single cream
- 3½ measures cola
- drinking chocolate powder, to decorate

Made with coffee beans and vanilla, Kahlúa is a rum-based liqueur from Mexico. It has a sweet and intense coffee flavour.

Put some ice cubes into a highball glass. Pour in the tequila, Kahlúa and cream, then top up with the cola. Stir gently and serve decorated with drinking chocolate powder.

BRAVE BULL

- ice cubes
- ¾ measure tequila
- ¾ measure Kahlúa

Fill a rocks glass with ice cubes. Pour in the tequila and Kahlúa and stir gently.

DESERT DAISY

- crushed ice
- 1 measure tequila
- 1¼ measures fresh lime juice
- 2 teaspoons sugar syrup (see page 122)
- 1 tablespoon Fraise de Bois
- blackberry and strawberry, lime and orange wedges and mint sprig, to decorate

The delicious liqueur Fraise de Bois, which is made with tiny alpine or wild strawberries, is used in this cocktail.

Half-fill a large rocks glass with crushed ice. Pour in the tequila, lime juice and sugar syrup and stir gently until a frost forms. Add more crushed ice then float the Fraise de Bois on top (see page 36). Decorate with a blackberry, a strawberry, a lime wedge, an orange wedge and a mint sprig.

PINK CADILLAC CONVERTIBLE (Pictured)

- 3 lime wedges
- fine sea salt
- ice cubes
- 1¼ measures gold tequila
- ½ measure cranberry juice
- ¾ measure Grand Marnier
- lime wedge, to decorate

Frost the rim of a large rocks glass by moistening with a lime wedge, then pressing into salt (see page 144). Fill the glass with ice cubes. Pour the tequila and cranberry juice into a cocktail shaker. Squeeze over the juice from the remaining lime wedges, pressing the rind to release its oils. Drop the wedges into the shaker. Add 4–5 ice cubes and shake vigorously for 10 seconds, then strain into the glass. Drizzle the Grand Marnier over the top and decorate with lime wedges.

TEQUINI

- ice cubes
- 3 dashes orange bitters
- 3 measures tequila
- 2 teaspoons dry French vermouth, preferably Noilly Prat
- 3 large black olives, to decorate

This is the Mexican equivalent of a Martini, with tequila replacing the gin and the orange bitters adding an exotic tang.

Fill a mixing glass with ice cubes. Add the bitters and tequila and stir gently for 10 seconds. Pour the vermouth into a chilled Martini glass, swirl around to coat the inside of the glass and then tip out. Stir the bitters and tequila for a further 10 seconds, then strain into the glass. Decorate with the olives and serve.

SLOE TEQUILA

- ice cubes
- 1 measure tequila
- 2 tablespoons sloe gin
- 2 tablespoons fresh lime juice
- cucumber peel spiral, to decorate

Put some ice cubes with the tequila, sloe gin and lime juice into a cocktail shaker and shake well. Strain into a Martini glass and fill up with ice cubes. Decorate with the cucumber peel spiral.

MARGARITA (Pictured)

- 1 lime wedge
- rock salt
- ice cubes
- 2 measures Herrudura Reposado Tequila
- 1 measure fresh lime juice
- 1 measure triple sec
- lime wheel to decorate

The exact origin of this famous drink is unknown. One story tells of a showgirl who was allergic to all alcohol except tequila. She asked a bartender to create her a cocktail with the spirit and the rest is history.

Moisten the rim of a Margarita glass with the lime wedge and frost with the salt (see page 144). Half-fill a cocktail shaker with ice cubes. Add all the remaining ingredients and shake until a frost forms on the outside of the shaker. Strain into the glass. Decorate with a lime wheel and serve.

STRAWBERRY MARGARITA

- 1 scoop crushed ice
- 1 measure tequila
- 1 measure triple sec
- 1 measure strawberry liqueur
- 1 measure fresh lime juice
- 12 strawberries, plus extra sliced strawberries to decorate

Put the crushed ice into a blender. Add all the remaining ingredients and blend on high speed until smooth but slushy. Pour into a chilled Margarita glass. Decorate with sliced strawberries and serve.

COBALT MARGARITA

- 1 lime wedge
- fine sea salt
- 4–5 ice cubes
- 1¼ measures tequila
- 2 teaspoons Cointreau
- ½ measure blue Curaçao
- ¾ measure fresh lime juice
- ¾ measure fresh grapefruit juice
- lime rind spiral, to decorate

It's the addition of blue Curaçao that gives this Margarita variation its name. The orange flavour of the Cointreau and the Curaçao blend with the grapefruit juice for a citrus hit.

Moisten the rim of a chilled Margarita glass with the lime wedge and frost with the salt (see page 144). Put the ice cubes into a cocktail shaker. Add all the remaining ingredients and shake until a frost forms on the outside of the shaker. Strain into the glass. Decorate with a lime rind spiral and serve.

GRAND MARGARITA

- 1 lime wedge, plus an extra to decorate
- rock salt
- ice cubes
- 1½ measures silver tequila
- 1 measure Grand Marnier
- 1 measure fresh lime juice

Moisten the rim of a Margarita glass with the lime wedge and frost with the salt (see page 144). Half-fill a cocktail shaker with ice cubes. Add all the remaining ingredients and shake until a frost forms on the outside of the shaker. Fine or double strain (see page 66) into the glass and decorate with an extra lime wedge.

CADILLAC

- 3 lime wedges
- fine sea salt
- 1¼ measures tequila gold
- ½ measure Cointreau
- 1¼ measures fresh lime juice
- 4–5 ice cubes
- 2 teaspoons Grand Marnier
- lime slice, to decorate

The Cadillac derives its name from the fact that it is a Margarita made only with the finest ingredients.

Frost the rim of a chilled Martini glass by moistening with a lime wedge, then pressing into the salt (see page 144). Pour the tequila, Cointreau and lime juice into a cocktail shaker. Squeeze over the juice from the remaining lime wedges, pressing the rind to release its oils. Drop the wedges into the shaker. Add the ice cubes and shake vigorously for 10 seconds, then strain into the prepared glass. Drizzle the Grand Marnier over the top and decorate with a lime slice.

RUBY RITA (Pictured)

- 1¼ measures fresh pink grapefruit juice
- fine sea salt
- ice cubes
- 1¼ measures tequila gold
- ¾ measure Cointreau
- pink grapefruit wedge, to decorate

Frost the rim of a rocks glass by moistening with some of the pink grapefruit juice and pressing into salt (see page 144). Fill the glass with ice cubes. Pour the tequila, Cointreau and the remaining pink grapefruit juice into a cocktail shaker, fill with more ice and shake vigorously. Strain into the prepared glass and decorate with a pink grapefruit wedge.

BATANGA

- 1 lime
- rock salt
- ice cubes
- 2 measures Tequileno Blanco tequila
- cola, to top up

This much-loved cocktail was invented by Don Javier Delgado Corona in his bar in Tequila, Mexico in 1961. Batanga was the nickname of one of his friends.

Cut the tip off the lime and make a slit in its side. Dip in the salt and run it around the edge of a rocks glass. Fill the glass with ice cubes and add the tequila. Squeeze out half the lime juice, then with the knife used to cut the lime, stir the drink while topping up with cola.

EL DIABLO

- ice cubes
- 1¼ measures gold tequila
- ¾ measure fresh lime juice
- 2 teaspoons grenadine
- 4 measures ginger ale
- lime wheel, to decorate

Fill a highball glass with ice cubes. Pour over the tequila, lime juice and grenadine. Top up with ginger ale and stir gently. Decorate with a lime wheel and serve.

PRETTY AS A PITCHER

So, you've chosen the right glass, you've measured out the spirits accurately and you've poured the drink without spilling a drop. Now it's time to add the finishing touches to your cocktail creation. Many drinks come served with a decoration and it's a chance for bartenders to show off their creative leanings by manipulating fruit into weird and wonderful shapes or frosting the glass. Here are a few ideas to wow your guests.

FROSTING

Some cocktails (such as the Margarita) require frosting as part of the recipe, while others can be frosted purely for decoration. You can use either salt, sugar or sometimes cocoa powder, and it's an easy technique to perfect.

- Put some lemon or lime juice or water into a saucer and dip the rim of the glass into it.
- Now dip the glass into the sugar or salt (again, using a saucer), twisting it around for even coverage.
- Clean excess frosting from the inside of the glass using a lime or lemon wedge.
- Carefully pour the drink into the centre of the glass so that the frosting remains intact.

FRUIT WEDGES

This is the classic cocktail accompaniment and it works with any citrus fruit. Sometimes the drink will call for a particular wedge, otherwise use your discretion. But remember, less is more – if you can't get to the drink for a forest of fruit decorations, then you've probably taken it a step too far. You can either balance the lemon or lime wedge on top of the drink, or you can use it to decorate the rim of the glass.

WHEELS

As the name suggest, these are neat, thin cross-sections of citrus fruit. Again, you can either float a lemon or lime wheel on the drink itself, or cut through to the middle of the citrus wheel and sit it on the rim of the glass.

CITRUS TWISTS

This one is for flavour, as well as aesthetics, and some recipes call for a twist of orange or lemon rind to be to be added at the end.

- Pare a wide strip of rind from the fruit, remove all traces of pith and give it it a quick twist over the drink to release the aroma and then drop it on top.

FRUIT KEBABS

You can go as crazy as you like with these decorations, which look fabulous.

- Use any small fruit you like – blueberries, cranberries, red currants, strawberries – and thread them onto a cocktail stick.
- Balance the stick on the edge of the glass to finish off the drink in style.

SPIRALS

Made from citrus fruit or cucumber, these require a little more time and attention than wedges and wheels, but they look impressive and you can always make a batch in advance.

- Cut a long, even strip of rind from a citrus fruit or cucumber and then wind it carefully around a straw or a bar spoon.
- Wait a minute or two for the spiral shape to set and then slide it off the straw and place it in the drink.

PINEAPPLE LEAVES

Just the thing to add a flourish of tropical style to cocktails like the Piña Colada, these are easy to prepare.

- Slice the bottom from a pineapple leaf then slice the leaf in half from the base to halfway along its length.
- Place the leaf upright on the edge of a highball or hurricane glass as a decoration.

MARACUJA (Pictured)

- 4–5 ice cubes
- 1 ripe passion fruit
- 1¼ measures gold tequila
- 1 tablespoon Creole Shrub
- ¾ measure fresh lime juice
- 2 teaspoons Cointreau
- 1 teaspoon passion fruit syrup
- physalis (Cape gooseberry), to decorate

Creole Shrub is an attractive golden-coloured rum, which is flavoured with orange rind. It is important to use a really ripe passion fruit for this drink.

Put the ice cubes into a cocktail shaker. Halve the passion fruit and scoop out the flesh into the shaker. Add all the remaining ingredients and shake until a frost forms on the outside of the shaker. Fine or double strain (see page 66) into a chilled Martini glass. Decorate with a physalis and serve.

DIRTY SANCHEZ

- ice cubes
- 2 teaspoons Noilly Prat
- 2 measures gold tequila, preferably Anejo
- 2 teaspoons brine from a jar of black olives
- 2 black olives, to decorate

Fill a mixing glass with ice cubes and add the vermouth. Stir to coat the ice, then discard the excess vermouth. Add the tequila and brine and stir until thoroughly chilled. Strain into a chilled Martini glass and decorate with black olives.

ACAPULCO

- ice cubes
- 1 measure tequila
- 1 measure white rum
- 2 measures pineapple juice
- 1 measure fresh grapefruit juice
- 1 measure coconut syrup
- pineapple wedge, to decorate

Another classic combination of ingredients – this time, it's rum and coconut – makes its way into this exotic cocktail. This drink takes its name from the Mexican party town.

Crack 4–5 ice cubes and put into a cocktail shaker. Fill a highball glass with ice cubes. Add all the remaining ingredients to the shaker and shake until a frost forms on the outside of the shaker. Strain over the ice in the glass. Decorate with a pineapple wedge and serve with straws.

PANCHO VILLA

- 4–5 ice cubes
- 1 measure tequila
- ½ measure Tia Maria
- 1 teaspoon Cointreau

Put the ice cubes into a cocktail shaker and pour in the tequila, Tia Maria and Cointreau. Shake until a frost forms, then strain into a chilled Martini glass.

RUDE COSMOPOLITAN

- ice cubes
- 1½ measures gold tequila
- 1 measure Cointreau
- 1 measure cranberry juice
- ½ measure fresh lime juice
- flamed orange rind twist, to decorate

To make the flamed orange twist to decorate this drink, pare a large strip of orange rind (see page 145), hold it over the glass with one hand and hold a long, lighted match or candle in the other hand. Twist the rind firmly so that the oils spray into the flame and ignite onto the drink.

Put the ice cubes into a cocktail shaker. Add all the remaining ingredients and shake until a frost forms on the outside of the shaker. Strain into a chilled Martini glass. Decorate with a flamed orange rind twist and serve.

FROSTBITE

- 4–5 ice cubes
- 1 measure tequila
- 1 measure double cream
- 1 measure white crème de cacao
- ½ measure white crème de menthe
- drinking chocolate powder, to decorate

Put the ice cubes into a cocktail shaker. Pour in the tequila, cream, crème de cacao and crème de menthe and shake vigorously for 10 seconds. Strain into a chilled Martini glass. Sprinkle with drinking chocolate powder.

FLAT LINER

- ¾ measure gold tequila
- 4 drops Tabasco sauce
- ¾ measure Sambuca

Featured in this cocktail is Sambuca, which is a clear liqueur flavoured with essential oils from star anise, liquorice and other herbs.

First pour the tequila into a shot glass. Using the back of a bar spoon, slowly float the Tabasco over the tequila (see page 36). Pour the Sambuca over the Tabasco in the same way.

PALE ORIGINAL (Pictured)

- 1 scoop crushed ice
- 2 measures gold tequila
- 1 measure fresh lime juice
- 2 teaspoons ginger syrup
- 1 measure guava juice
- grated lime rind,
  to decorate

Put the crushed ice into a blender. Add all the remaining ingredients and blend on high speed until slushy. Pour into a large Margarita glass. Decorate with grated lime rind and serve.

BRANDY

BRANDY ALEXANDER (Pictured)

- 3 ice cubes, cracked
- 1 measure brandy
- 1 measure dark crème de cacao
- 1 measure single cream
- chocolate flake, to decorate

A sweet and creamy after-dinner cocktail with a chocolate aftertaste. Use ice cream instead of cream, blend well and you have a Frozen Alexander.

Put the cracked ice into a cocktail shaker. Add all the remaining ingredients and shake until a frost forms on the outside of the shaker. Strain into a chilled Martini glass. Decorate with a sprinkling of chocolate flake and serve.

BRANDY FIX

- crushed ice
- 2 teaspoons sugar syrup (see page 122)
- 1¼ measures fresh lemon juice
- ½ measure cherry brandy
- 1 measure brandy
- lemon rind spiral, to decorate

Fill a rocks glass with crushed ice. Build all the ingredients, one by one in order, over the ice. Decorate the cocktail with a lemon rind spiral and serve.

BRANDY SIDECAR

- ice cubes
- 1 measure Cointreau
- 2 measures brandy
- 1 measure fresh lemon juice
- maraschino cherry and orange rind spiral, to decorate

This drink was reputedly created at the Ritz Hotel in Paris during World War I for one of the bar's regulars, an army captain who travelled in a motorbike sidecar.

Half-fill a cocktail shaker with ice cubes. Add all the remaining ingredients and shake until a frost forms on the outside of the shaker. Strain into a chilled Martini glass. Decorate with a maraschino cherry on a cocktail stick and an orange rind spiral and serve.

SHANGHAI

- 3 ice cubes, crushed
- 1 measure brandy
- ½ measure Curaçao
- ¼ measure maraschino liqueur
- 2 dashes Angostura bitters
- lemon rind spiral and cocktail cherry, to decorate

Put the crushed ice into a cocktail shaker. Add the brandy, Curaçao, maraschino and bitters and shake to mix. Pour into a Martini glass and decorate with a lemon rind spiral and a cherry impaled on a cocktail stick.

PARISIEN (Pictured)

- crushed ice
- 1 measure brandy
- ½ measure Calvados
- 1 measure fresh lemon juice
- sugar syrup, to taste (see page 122)
- ½ measure Poire William
- apple and pear slices, to decorate

This cocktail includes Calvados, an apple brandy from the French region of Lower Normandy. It is made from specially grown apples, both sweet and tart varieties.

Fill a glass with crushed ice. Add the brandy, Calvados, lemon juice and sugar syrup to taste. Pour the Poire William over the top and decorate with apple and pear slices.

SCORPION

- 5 ice cubes, crushed
- 1 measure brandy
- ½ measure white rum
- ½ measure dark rum
- 2 measures fresh orange juice
- 2 teaspoons Amaretto di Saronno
- 2–3 dashes Angostura bitters
- orange or lemon slices, to decorate

Put half the crushed ice into a cocktail shaker and add the brandy, rums, orange juice, Amaretto and bitters. Shake until a frost forms. Strain over the remaining ice in a tall glass. Decorate with orange or lemon slices and serve with a straw.

LEO

- 2–3 ice cubes, crushed
- 1 measure brandy
- 1½ measures fresh orange juice
- ½ measure Amaretto di Saronno
- soda water, to taste
- 1 teaspoon Campari

Campari is dark red aperitif which has as its essential ingredient *chinotto* oranges. Also known as myrtle-leaved oranges, these are small bitter oranges grown in specific regions of Italy.

Put the crushed ice into a cocktail shaker. Add the brandy, orange juice and Amaretto and shake well. Strain into a tall glass and add soda water to taste and the Campari.

BRANDY SOUR

- 4–5 ice cubes
- 3 drops Angostura bitters
- juice of ½ lemon
- 3 measures brandy
- 1 teaspoon sugar syrup (see page 122)
- lemon slices, to decorate

Put the ice cubes into a cocktail shaker. Shake the bitters over the ice, add the lemon juice, brandy and sugar syrup and shake until a frost forms. Strain over the remaining ice in a glass and decorate with lemon slices impaled on a cocktail stick. Serve with a straw.

AMERICAN BEAUTY (Pictured)

- 4–5 ice cubes
- 1 measure brandy
- 1 measure dry vermouth
- 1 measure fresh orange juice
- 1 measure grenadine
- 1 dash white crème de menthe
- 2–3 dashes ruby port
- maraschino cherries, mint and orange rind spiral, to decorate

Ruby port gets its name from its distinctive dark red colour. It's a fortified wine with brandy added to stop fermentation at a certain stage so that the alcohol content is higher than regular wine.

Put the ice cubes into a cocktail shaker. Add the brandy, vermouth, orange juice, grenadine and crème de menthe and shake until a frost forms on the outside of the shaker. Strain into a Martini glass. Tilt the glass and gently pour in the port so it floats on top (see page 36). Decorate with maraschino cherries, a mint sprig and an orange rind spiral and serve.

BEDTIME BOUNCER

- 2 measures brandy
- 1 measure Cointreau
- 5 measures bitter lemon
- 4–6 ice cubes
- lemon rind spiral, to decorate

Pour the brandy, Cointreau and bitter lemon into a rocks glass, stir well and add the ice. Decorate with a lemon rind spiral and serve with a straw.

BRANDY CRUSTA

- 1 lemon wedge
- caster sugar
- ice cubes
- 2 measures brandy
- ½ measure orange Curaçao
- ½ measure maraschino liqueur
- 1 measure fresh lemon juice
- 3 dashes Angostura bitters
- lemon rind spiral, to decorate

A Crusta combines a spirit with lemon juice and Angostura bitters and is traditionally served with a lemon rind spiral.

Moisten the rim of a chilled Martini glass with the lemon wedge and frost with the sugar (see page 144). Half-fill a cocktail shaker with ice cubes. Add all the remaining ingredients and shake until a frost forms on the outside of the shaker. Strain into the glass. Decorate with a lemon rind spiral and serve.

BOUNCING BOMB

- 4–5 ice cubes
- 2 measures brandy
- 1 measure Curaçao
- soda water, to top up
- orange rind strip,
  to decorate

Put the ice cubes into a mixing glass. Pour the brandy and Curaçao over the ice and stir vigorously. Strain into a highball glass and top up with soda water. Decorate the cocktail with an orange rind strip.

NICE PEAR (Pictured)

- ice cubes
- 2 measures brandy
- 1 measure Poire William
- 1 measure sweet vermouth
- pear slices, to decorate

The pear flavour of this cocktail comes from Poire William, which is a colourless brandy made from the Williams, or Bartlett, pear.

Half-fill a cocktail shaker with ice cubes. Add all the remaining ingredients and shake until a frost forms on the outside of the shaker. Strain into a chilled Martini glass. Decorate with pear slices and serve.

BRANDY CLASSIC

- ice cubes, cracked
- 1 measure brandy
- 1 measure blue Curaçao
- 1 measure maraschino liqueur
- juice of ½ lemon
- lemon wedge, to decorate

Put 4–5 cracked ice cubes into a cocktail shaker. Add all the remaining ingredients and shake briefly to mix. Strain into a chilled Martini glass. Add some more cracked ice, decorate with a lemon wedge and serve.

BETWEEN THE SHEETS

- ice cubes
- ½ measure brandy
- ½ measure white rum
- ½ measure Cointreau
- 1 measure fresh orange juice
- orange rind spiral, to decorate

An orange-flavoured drink that delivers a powerful punch. White rum has a much lighter flavour than dark rum, complementing the flavour of the Cointreau and brandy.

Half-fill a cocktail shaker with ice cubes. Add all the remaining ingredients and shake briefly to mix. Strain into a chilled Martini glass. Decorate with an orange rind spiral and serve.

METROPOLITAN

- ice cubes, cracked
- 1 measure brandy
- 1 measure sweet vermouth
- ½ teaspoon sugar syrup (see page 122)
- 3–4 dashes Angostura bitters

Half-fill a cocktail shaker with cracked ice. Add all the remaining ingredients and shake until a frost forms on the outside of the shaker. Strain into a chilled Martini glass and serve.

JAFFA

- ice cubes
- 1 measure brandy
- 1 measure dark crème de cacao
- 1 measure single cream
- ½ measure Mandarine Napoléon
- 2 dashes orange bitters
- orange-flavoured chocolate shavings, to decorate

This cocktail takes its name from a variety of orange. As it includes Mandarine Napoléon, orange bitters and chocolate-orange shavings, it's not hard to see why!

Half-fill a cocktail shaker with ice cubes. Add all the remaining ingredients and shake until a frost forms on the outside of the shaker. Strain into a chilled Martini glass. Decorate with orange-flavoured chocolate shavings and serve.

TIDAL WAVE (Pictured)

- 6 ice cubes
- 1 measure Mandarine Napoléon
- 4 measures bitter lemon
- 1 dash fresh lemon juice
- lemon slice, to decorate

Put the ice cubes into a highball glass. Add the Mandarine Napoléon, bitter lemon and lemon juice and stir well. Decorate with a lemon slice.

BRANDY FLIP

- ice cubes
- 1 egg
- 2 measures brandy
- 1½ teaspoons caster sugar
- freshly grated nutmeg, to decorate

A flip is a spirit or wine shaken with egg and sugar until frothy, then dusted with nutmeg. Early flips were warmed by plunging a red-hot poker into the drink.

Half-fill a cocktail shaker with ice cubes. Add all the remaining ingredients and shake until a frost forms on the outside of the shaker. Strain into a balloon glass. Decorate with a little grated nutmeg and serve.

APPLE POSSET

- 8 measures unsweetened apple juice
- 1 teaspoon soft brown sugar
- 2 tablespoons Calvados
- cinnamon stick

Heat the apple juice in a small saucepan to just below boiling point. Meanwhile, measure the sugar and Calvados into a warmed glass or mug. Pour the hot apple juice on to the sugar and Calvados, stirring with the cinnamon stick until the sugar has dissolved, and serve.

OTHER WINES
AND SPIRITS

BLACK VELVET (Pictured)

- 5 measures Guinness
- 5 measures Champagne

This famous cocktail was created by a bartender at Brooks's Club in London in 1861 to mark the death of Prince Albert. If cider or perry are used instead of Champagne, it becomes a Poor Man's Black Velvet.

Pour the Guinness into a champagne glass. Carefully add the Champagne, then serve.

SANGRIA

Serves 10–12

- ice cubes
- 2 bottles light Spanish red wine, chilled
- 4 measures brandy (optional)
- 450ml (¾ pint) soda water, chilled
- fruit in season, such as apples, pears, lemons, peaches and strawberries, sliced
- orange slices, to decorate

Put some ice cubes into a large bowl and pour over the wine and brandy, if using. Stir. Add the soda water and float the fruit on top. Serve in tall glasses and decorate with orange slices.

CAIPIRINHA

- 1 lime, quartered
- 2 teaspoons caster sugar
- crushed ice
- 2 measures cachaça

This is by far the most famous of Brazilian cocktails, whose main ingredient is the local liquor, cachaça, of which over 4,000 brands are available.

Put the lime quarters and sugar into a rocks glass and muddle together (see page 37). Fill the glass with crushed ice and pour over the cachaça. Stir and add more ice as desired.

WHITE SANGRIA

Serves 6

- 2 large glasses dry white wine
- 2 measures lemon vodka
- 2 measures peach schnapps
- 2 measures peach purée
- apple, lime, lemon and peach slices
- ice cubes
- 1 measure fresh lemon juice
- 1 measure fresh lime juice
- lemonade, to top up

Twelve hours before serving, put the wine, vodka, schnapps, peach purée and fruit slices into a jug and stir to mix. Cover and chill in the refrigerator. Just before serving, add some ice cubes and the fruit juices and top up with lemonade. Serve from the jug into rocks glasses.

PISCO SOUR (Pictured)

- ice cubes
- 2 measures Pisco
- 1 measure fresh lemon juice
- 2 teaspoons caster sugar
- 1 egg white
- dash Angostura bitters

First created in the early 1900s, this cocktail came about to render Pisco, a grape brandy often of a low quality, more drinkable with a simple sweet and sour mix.

Half-fill a cocktail shaker with ice cubes and fill a large wine goblet with ice cubes. Add the Pisco, lemon juice, sugar and egg white to the shaker and shake until a frost forms on the outside of the shaker. Strain over the ice in the glass. Add the bitters to the drink's frothy head and serve.

CHAMPAGNE COCKTAIL

- 1 white sugar cube
- 1–2 dashes Angostura bitters
- 1 measure brandy
- 4 measures chilled Champagne
- orange wheel, to decorate

Put the sugar cube into a chilled Martini glass or Champagne flute and saturate with the bitters. Add the brandy, then top up with the chilled Champagne. Decorate with an orange wheel and serve.

PIMM'S COCKTAIL

- ice cubes
- 1 measure Pimm's No 1
- 1 measure gin
- 2 measures lemonade
- 2 measures ginger ale
- cucumber strips, blueberries and orange wheels, to decorate

Pimm's No 1 was introduced by James Pimm in 1823 at his oyster bar in the City of London as a more flavourful alternative to the neat gin commonly served with oysters at that time.

Fill a highball glass with ice cubes. Build all the remaining ingredients, one by one in order, over the ice. Decorate with cucumber strips, blueberries and orange wheels and serve.

CHAMPAGNE JULEP

- 3 mint sprigs
- 1 tablespoon sugar syrup (see page 122)
- crushed ice
- 1 measure brandy
- Champagne, to top up

Put 2 mint sprigs and the sugar syrup into a highball glass and muddle together (see page 37). Fill the glass with crushed ice, then add the brandy. Top up with Champagne and stir gently. Decorate with a mint sprig, then serve.

LONG ISLAND ICED TEA (Pictured)

- ice cubes
- ½ measure vodka
- ½ measure gin
- ½ measure white rum
- ½ measure tequila
- ½ measure Cointreau
- ½ measure fresh lemon juice
- cola, to top up
- lemon wedge, to decorate

A very potent brew, supposedly created by Robert 'Rosebud' Butt of the Oak Beach Inn, Hampton Bay.

Half-fill a cocktail shaker with ice cubes and fill a highball glass with ice cubes. Add the vodka, gin, rum, tequila, Cointreau and lemon juice to the shaker and briefly shake to mix. Strain over the ice in the glass. Top up with cola. Decorate with a lemon wedge and serve.

GRAND MIMOSA

- 1 measure Grand Marnier
- 2 measures fresh orange juice
- Champagne, to top up

Pour the Grand Marnier and orange juice into a Champagne flute and top up with chilled Champagne.

BATIDA

- crushed ice
- 2 measures cachaça
- ½ measure sugar syrup (see page 122)
- ½ measure fresh lemon juice
- 3 measures fresh fruit juice, such as strawberry, pineapple or mango

Batidas are popular Brazilian cocktails blended from fresh fruit juice and cachaça. The most common variations in Brazil include passion fruit, coconut milk and cashew fruit.

Fill a highball glass with crushed ice. Pour the cachaça, sugar syrup, lemon juice and fruit juice into the glass and stir to mix thoroughly.

RITZ FIZZ I

- 1 dash blue Curaçao
- 1 dash fresh lemon juice
- 1 dash Amaretto di Saronno
- Champagne, to top up
- lemon rind spiral, to decorate

Pour the Curaçao, lemon juice and Amaretto into a glass and top up with Champagne. Stir gently to mix and decorate with a lemon rind spiral.

SAKE-TINI

- ice cubes
- 2½ measures sake
- 1 measure vodka
- ½ measure orange Curaçao
- 2 thin cucumber wheels, to decorate

Recorded as existing as early as the third century AD, sake is a Japanese liquor made with rice. Although it is often referred to as a wine, sake is brewed in a similar way to beer.

Put the ice cubes into a mixing glass, add the sake, vodka and Curaçao and stir well. Strain into a chilled Martini glass and add two cucumber wheels, made by peeling the cucumber in strips, lengthwise and then thinly slicing.

FLAMING LAMBORGHINI

- 1 measure Kahlúa
- 1 measure Sambuca
- 1 measure Baileys Irish Cream
- 1 measure blue Curaçao

Pour the Kahlúa into a warmed Martini glass. Gently pour half a measure of Sambuca over the back of a spoon into the Martini glass, so that it floats on top (see page 36). Pour the Baileys and the blue Curaçao into 2 short glasses. Next, pour the remaining Sambuca into a warmed wine glass and carefully set it alight. Pour it into the Martini glass with care. Pour the Baileys and Curaçao into the lighted Martini glass at the same time. Serve with a straw.

B-52 (Pictured)

- ½ measure Kahlúa
- ½ measure Baileys Irish Cream
- ½ measure Grand Marnier

The B-52 is an iconic layered cocktail which was invented in the 1970s and is named after the B-52 Stratofortress long-range bomber used by the United States in the Vietnam War.

Pour the Kahlúa into a shot glass. Using the back of a bar spoon, slowly float the Baileys over the Kahlúa (see page 36). Pour the Grand Marnier over the Baileys in the same way.

SLIPPERY NIPPLE

- 1 measure Sambuca
- ½ measure Baileys Irish Cream

Pour the Sambuca into a shot glass. Using the back of a bar spoon, slowly float the Baileys over the Sambuca (see page 36).

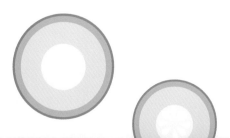

GLOSSARY

Aperitif

Term for an alcoholic beverage that is drunk before a meal in order to stimulate the palate.

Blend

It is sometimes necessary to blend a cocktail that uses fresh fruit or crushed ice. Add your ingredients to an electric blender or liquidizer, usually along with crushed or cracked ice, and blend for about 10 seconds. Never add carbonated liquids to a blender, as the mixture might explode.

Build

A term used to describe the simplest cocktail-making process, in which you fill the glass with ice and pour over the ingredients, in the correct order and proportion, and serve.

Dash

A very small amount of an ingredient added to a cocktail, approximately 5 ml (1 teaspoon). A term usually used in relation to ingredients with a very strong flavour, such as syrups, bitters and sauces.

Float

To form a separate layer of liquid on top of a second, denser liquid ingredient in a drink, gently pour the liquid over the back of a spoon, making sure the spoon is touching the inside of the glass and is in contact with the drink. A float is often achieved by using a bar spoon, as in the technique of layering (see page 36).

Frappé

A chilled cocktail poured over finely crushed ice, often served with a straw so that the drink and ice can be sipped together from the bottom of the glass.

Frosting

An effect achieved by coating the rim of a cocktail glass, usually with sugar or salt (see page 36). The best-known example of this is the Margarita. Wet the rim of the glass with water or egg white, then dip it in your chosen coating.

Muddling

A technique in which you use a blunt tool, known as a muddler, to mash fruit, herbs and syrups together in the bottom of a glass at the beginning of the cocktail-making process. This is done to release their juices and extract as much flavour as possible from the ingredients.

Neat

A drink served without ice or a mixer.

On the rocks

A drink served over ice cubes, which serves to chill the liquor as well as diluting it slightly, but at a much slower rate than if you were using crushed ice.

Shaking

The art of mixing and chilling a cocktail in one action (see page 35): all the ingredients are added to a cocktail shaker along with cubed or cracked ice and shaken vigorously. As well as chilling the drink, the ice acts as a beater in the shaker.

Spiral

A decoration made by cutting a long strip of rind from a citrus fruit and winding it around a cylindrical shape, such as a straw, to give it a spiral shape. This citrus spiral can be added to a drink to give it extra flavour, as well as decorating the cocktail.

Stirring

As a general rule, cocktails featuring transparent ingredients are stirred rather than shaken, as vigorous shaking would spoil the drink's clarity. Place the ingredients, in the order stated in the recipe, in a mixing glass or serving glass. Stir gently with a long-handled spool, then strain into a fresh glass if required.

Straight up

A drink served without the addition of ice, usually in a tall glass.

Straining

After a cocktail has been shaken or stirred, it is often strained to remove ice and fruit fragments. The strainer can come as part of a standard cocktail shaker set. Some cocktails that must be served absolutely clear require a double straining using a second fine strainer fitted over the glass.

Swizzle stick

An implement that has a double use as stirrer and decoration, often used to prevent ingredients settling at the bottom of a glass.

Twist

A long piece of pared fruit, usually taken from a citrus fruit, which is added to a drink to release the oils and impart flavour.

INDEX

PICTURE CREDITS